Dominate Your Competition

5 Proven Steps to Differentiate Your Business in Your Marketplace

Achille Nangbong B. Bomboma

Christopher D. McMullan

Founders of wEquipu, LLC

Dominate Your Competition

5 Proven Steps to Differentiate Your Business in Your Marketplace

ISBN – 978-1-7345336-0-6

Part of the proceeds of this book will go to international business educational projects. Contact our office for additional information.
Info@wEquipu.com
https://wequipuseo.com
https://wequipu.com

To download our digital forms mentioned in this book, visit
5provenstepstodifferentiateyourbusinesses.com
Book Cover design - Ichane Tchadjobo
Freddy Kodjo N'tsougnon

ACKNOWLEDGEMENTS

Our gratitude goes to all our clients who participated at different levels to this journey especially:

Wisdom Senior Care

Wisdom Health Academy

Mr Laundromat

Right Time Kids

KroCia Wardrobe Consulting

Third Degree Solutions

Behold Roofing

West Alley BBQ

Infuzion Foods

Neat Clean Services

Carlos Brown Law

Law Office Of Rebekah S. Bell

Vigor Biopharma Solutions

Birch Point Paper Products

GPX International Tire Sold to Yokohama Tire Corp

FOREWORD

Many years, I searched for solutions for my business. I tried marketing fads, purchased pointless programs and even spoke with gurus who told me that they knew what I was missing and they had all the answers. Nothing they said or did worked for me. I felt stuck.

If you don't know who you are and the audience you've been called to serve in business, you are doomed to run around in circles, looking for solutions in the wrong places from the wrong people. I was one of these people. I was content rich and had written numerous books. I was a seasoned communicator but my message was not resonating where I was standing. It was as if I was in a valley surrounded by mountains and my words were hitting the mountains and bouncing back and falling on the ground in around me.

Then one day, something unexpected happened. Achille Nangbong K. Bomboma asked me to help him with a book that he and his co-author and business partner Christopher McMullan had written. Since I had been a book coach for several years, I knew I could do what they wanted, but what I did not expect was that this project would actually serve as a gift to me.

When I read the title, I believed that it would be like many of the other business books I had read. Most people believe that they have all the answers when it comes to providing content and doing business. I would read some of these books and they said the same things. I believed that this was one of those books. I was in for a pleasant surprise. As a book coach and content editor, I have to read and reread books for clarity. As I worked on the project, I soon discovered that I was not only changing my language but also my mindset regarding my business. But the most important thing I discovered was that I was targeting the wrong audience with the wrong information. I believed that I was called to speak to everyone about everything but *Dominate Your Competition* changed that. I now know the identity of my ideal client and that has not only change my business model but also my bottom line!.

This book is filled with not only business changing information but the authors provide you with cases where they assisted actual clients in the implementing of their principles. The facts and figures are well documented and they have a list of happy clients who increased their market visibility and their bottom line.

Now, it's your turn to savor the message of this knowledge filled road map and dominate in your market. My hope is like me, you will be pleasantly surprised!

- Dr. Gail Hayes, CEO
The Handle Your Business Girl Empowerment Zone

TABLE OF CONTENTS

Section 5: Innovate Your Business page 156

Overview

Innovate Your Business

Example of Innovation Process

Assignment 7

INTRODUCTION

Are you ready to take your business to another level and dominate your market? Are you ready to have an overflow of satisfied customers who sing your praises and give you referrals? If you answered yes, then this book is for you. This easy to read guide gives you five simple steps broken into five sections to help you discover and understand some critical fundamentals required to build a successful business and dominate your market.

These proven steps work whether you are a new or seasoned entrepreneur, a business owner or even a politician running for office. That's right; we did say politician because running a successful campaign possesses the same facets as operating a successful business. It's all the same because creating a powerful brand and positioning it correctly in the marketplace makes the difference in either you getting elected or sitting in a coffee shop dreaming about your next bid for office.

We will give you the success template for business and should you choose to follow the template and honor the process, like many of our clients, you will make your business stand out in your chosen market. This template shows you how to create a market dominating position and takes you on a step-by-step guided tour to assist you in creating and carrying out this often neglected, critically important facet of your business.

"If it looks like a duck, walks like a duck and quacks like a duck, then it's a duck". - Unknown

Although the first printed example of this saying is thought to be from a 19th century American poet, legend says that people were using it as early as the 18th century, referring to a certain mechanical duck. The inventor of this mechanical duck built it to impress audiences of his day. The duck actually quacked and moved its head "to eat" grain and appeared to actually digest the grain. After a few minutes, the duck would then turn and "poop" out the grain in the form of a foul smelling dollop.

So what does this have to do with your business? Everything! You do not want to look, talk, and act like your competition. You are not mechanical. You are a creator and an original so you want to stand out by offering something unique and authentic. In other words, if your business looks, sounds, and acts like your competition, then you can be forever doomed to compete on price and the foul stench of failure could strangle your business.

You must be able to separate your business from your competition if you want to dominate your market. This means you must create a market dominating position and evolve your business in the process. Let's take a look at what we will cover.

In **Section One**, you will discover how to:

- Differentiate your business from your competition choosing strategic positioning
- Stake out a "market dominating position" for your business
- Discover five ways to separate your business from all others in your industry
- Learn the three categories that will make your business unique
- Learn the secrets of not using price to differentiate yourself

In **Section Two**, with the help of your customers' physical profile discovery, you should have a clearly defined profile of the physical characteristics that define your target customer. Unfortunately, the physical profile doesn't provide us with the complete picture. In fact, we consider the physical characteristics to be about 10% to 20% of
the picture. The remaining 80% to 90% are made up of what we call the emotional components or emotional triggers.

In **Section Three**, you will discover tools and approaches that highlight a key component in helping identifying your target customer emotional profile. Where the physical profile makes up the physical components that describe your target customer, the emotional profile defines the emotional components. This identifies in the "available universe" of prospects that **need** what you sell, those that **want** what you sell.

The content of this section is designed to help you to:

•Determine the emotional traits of your target prospects

•Identify the general emotional characteristics of your target customer

Know "what words to use" with your target prospects when preparing your marketing program. With the help of the physical and emotional profile discoveries, you will have a clearly defined profile of the characteristics that define your target customer. Please remember that the physical characteristics make up about 10% to 20% of the success equation for business startups. The remaining 80% to 90% are made up of the emotional components. Now comes the critically important part.

After finding your business purpose, you will need to list the specific emotions and define what your target customers really want. You then need to select the emotion that most resonates with your passion and make that focus your "niche" market.

In **Section 4**, you will define what separates your business from your competition. Selecting your niche market means you are now electing to **stop** being all things to all prospects. Once you grasp this concept, you can create a business that is "unique". This section will provide you with information that highlights another key component in identifying your target customer in relation to your purpose. The content of this section is designed to help you to:

• Select the top emotional traits from your list that you are most passionate about and that drive your purpose

- Build a business that is truly unique from your competitors by leveraging on your passion.
- Understand the importance of selecting and combining different offerings of multiple products and services.
- Redefine your physical profile traits to fit your specific niche market with your purpose and passion.
- Complete the process of building a business that is truly unique.

When you complete the first four sections, with the help of the physical and emotional profile studies, you should have a clearly defined profile of your target customers' characteristics. You should also have identified the one emotional trigger (emotional characteristic) or a combination of three that you feel most passionate about. That trigger or its combination will become your niche market and will enable you to dominate your market.

Once you select your "niche" market, you must then go back to your physical profile for review and revision. Your original physical profile identified the available universe of everyone who **needs** what you sell. That could be a larger group and also be just about anyone. With the selection of your specific niche market, you elect to serve a smaller segment of that universe; a universe that **wants** what you sell. It's important to review and redefine the physical profile of your target customer. You may discover it will narrow dramatically. This will make it easier to identify and market to your target customer.

At that point, you will be almost done developing your Target Customer Profile. This is one of the most important fundamentals in business today and an aspect that your competition usually overlooks. By completing this crucial first fundamental, you will position your business so that it is "unique". This is the first step toward separating your business from your competition and will assist you in your quest to dominate your market.

Once you complete this process, you will be ready to move into **Section Five**. This section is a critical step in business fundamentals that help to position your business as the only business in your industry that truly offers extraordinary value. In this section, you are going to:

•Identify the typical or specific emotional trigger your prospects experience within your niche market.
•Analyze whether you currently offer a solution for those needs and wants.
•Ask yourself what more can you do in the way of innovation that will make your business a no-brainer choice for your prospects.
•List all the benefits your prospects will experience once they use your innovations. This helps to create ongoing extraordinary value and compels your prospects to buy from you and you alone. In

fact, your prospects will quickly realize that they would be missing out if they buy what you sell from anyone else.

This book will be your "go to" guide and a vital component for your business success. It will be highly advantageous to take your time and glean from the contents and do the assignments. We developed and tested the content with small and medium sized businesses but these principles are still valuable for any business striving to position itself in the marketplace.

Now is the time to take **massive action** and apply these steps to your business. As you already know, if you do not have the right business mindset, discipline, determination and persistence, you won't get satisfactory results. We tested these steps and used them with our clients and we believe that they will work for you. They are proven results oriented steps that will not only help you to only dominate but will also help you develop an impacting marketing program.

Once you grasp the concepts in this book, you will be ready to speak to your prospects' hearts. You will be available to offer solutions and benefits through your products and services beyond their features. You can also get more information on improving your communication by contacting us to see how we can help you.

Understand and know that these concepts will work in almost any arena, including in the workplace and in your own business. Next

, we will explore the benefits of strategic positioning.

Introduction

SECTION ONE

Strategically Positioning Your Business

"The size of a ship doesn't stop it from sinking."

- African Proverb

SECTION ONE
Strategically Positioning Your Business

In this section, we begin the process of discovering ways to establish a market dominating position for your business. Most small to medium sized businesses usually establish themselves in response to demand for a product or service. Many build their businesses by serving that demand and enjoying some great growing profits without putting much effort into long term planning or marketing.

But what happens when that demand slows or even stops? What happens when the competition sets up shop with a new and improved version of your product down the road? How will you keep your offering fresh while growing and maintaining your client base? The answer - innovate your business and offer extraordinary value by creating a market dominating position.

Consider this, every choice you make when buying a product or service represents a point of differentiation between one company and their competitors. These differences, whether subtle or distinct, determine which customers will buy what you sell. Consider the well documented case of Domino's Pizza. Why and how did Domino's Pizza become a billion dollar behemoth in an overcrowded market in just a few years?

Did Domino's make the best pizza? Did they offer comfortable in-house dining? No way. Did they offer the largest selection on their menu? No, not even close. They offer the exact same pizza as all their competitors. What did they do differently to make themselves stand out and dominate their market? They did this by adopting and carrying out one and only one major strategy. They created a dominating position by providing fast, hot pizza specifically for hungry college students.

Now ask yourself, what makes your business different from your competitors? What do your customers experience that makes you stand out and become their preferred choice? For the vast majority of businesses, the answer is price. So, if that is true, then let's consider a few of today's top selling companies.

Nike offers a wide variety of shoe, apparel, and equipment products; all which are among global best sellers. The top selling Air Jordan 3 has an average price of over one hundred-fifty dollars, and yet Target sells an excellent imitation for around forty dollars. But the fact is that the Nike version outsells the Target shoe by more than ten to one. How is this possible?

Have you purchased coffee at Starbucks lately? Their typical customer spends between three dollars and fifty cents to four dollars on every visit. That price is around four times higher than their competitors and yet, customers do not mind standing in long lies for that hot cup of java. Looking at their example, it's obvious that low pricing is not the driving force behind their success.

So, what is the secret of these business giants? The answer is that these top selling companies staked out a specific and targeted market dominating position. For Nike, their position revolves around being the best athlete, being hip and in style along with their perception of quality. For Starbucks, it is their delicious beverages which they claim hold the secret to making life better. For Domino's it's fast, hot pizza for thirty minutes or less. What is it for you and your arena? If you do not know the answer, the next section should help.

What Exactly is a Marketing Dominating Position?

When you create your own strategic market dominating position, individuals and businesses will consistently choose your business over your competitor's. But what exactly is a market dominating position and how do you create it? It's simply any value added customer perceived benefit or a combination of benefits that differentiates you from your competitors. This position is so powerful that it makes your business appear as the only logical choice in the minds of your prospects and customers.

Here's another example is a dry cleaning business that offers pickup and delivery. This cleaner may not be the best in cleaning or the least expensive, but they offer an added value with pick up and delivery. This added value establishes them as the logical choice for many because of convenience. This simple distinction of premium service catapults them into a market dominating position. Their customers do not use them for price but rather for saving them time.

This is a clear example of how prospects and customers do not solely purchase just on pricing. They spend their money based on the value they receive for the price they pay. They pay for what they want and need. When you create added value to your business model, you add more customers. People love gifts and when you add to your original offering, a free gift or discounted package, you win every time. These bonuses attract new customers and help you to retain existing customers.

Another example of added value is a gift shop owner who offers complimentary gift wrapping. This is value is especially critical during holiday and gift giving season. This shop owner understands that once they offer this value, it must continue to be a part of what they offer. They understand that once they offer a value, they must revisit (for some it could mean upgrade or improve) the value and make it a consistent part of what they do, they may lose business.

In business, your customers expect added value. If you give them added value, they will not only always support your business but they will also send referrals if they like what you offer. They will only be drawn to your competitors if you are not consistent in your service. Ultimately your customers will demand additional value to remain loyal and they are the keystones for your business growth.

Adding value to your business doesn't have to monopolize your time or blow your marketing budget. There are many ways to enhance your business in the eyes of your clients. The key to adding value is determining what your target market perceives as value. In other words, you must "get inside their heads" and come to understand their needs and wants. You must also discover the

challenges and inconveniences they face so your added values become their solutions. Added value increases your business profits. This is a good when you make a part of every aspect of your business. It's critical that you always remember that profits will never be consistent unless service comes first. Service must be a critical facet of your business model. When you genuinely focus on helping your clients solve a problem or positively overcome a challenge, you will have no problem attracting and keeping them. Added value works for both product and service-based businesses.

For example, if you own a beauty salon, offer your clients a latte during their visit or complimentary shampoo samples. Give them something that makes their experiences appear to be one of luxury. This is especially true since coming to a salon is not a necessity. Clients come because they want the experience. They want to emerge from that chair feeling beautiful. How you make them feel is a critical part of the experience.

You can also develop a rewards program where your clients

receive free services after a certain number of visits. If you sell a product, consider offering convenience services like free shipping or delivery to ensure that your customers experience seamless appreciation. You can be as creative as you want to create a customer atmosphere of added value. It's your business so you get to bring the magic! Now, let's explore the five steps to strategic positioning.

Five Steps to Strategic Positioning

In order to distinguish your business from your competition, you must create strategic positioning that involves five critical steps. They are as follows:

Step One - Determine your strategic position in the market. What is your specific niche market or on what segment of the market does your business focus? Determining this involves combining the purpose of your business with the unmet needs of your target prospects. Once you identify your position, you must then design your product or service to fulfill those needs. Domino's strategic position was fast, hot pizza for hungry college students. For Starbucks, delicious handcrafted beverages that tasted good, but were also delivered fast and met the needs of busy professionals.

Step Two - Determine your primary market dominating position. This is the powerful advantage that separates you from your competitors. Domino's claimed it could deliver its pizza in 30 minutes or less or it would be free. This was the primary advantage that met the needs of their newly defined market position. Hungry college students wanted hot, food fast and Dominos delivered. Starbucks created drinks with "fresh" sounding names while adding exotic teas and coffee beverages to its menu. It was and still is a winning combination.

Step Three – Determine your supporting business model. How are you going to deliver what your strategic position and primary market dominating position promises? What changes, if any, do you need to make to ensure that your business delivers consistently on your position and promise? Domino's built a supporting business model that consistently enabled them to provide their promised primary advantage: fresh, hot pizza delivered within thirty minutes.

To make good on this promise every time, they created a supporting business model where they built low cost plain vanilla stores strategically located near college campuses. They also understood that they could not fully rely on college student employees, so they hired additional, stand by delivery staff from the community at large. These innovations allowed them to consistently meet and more often exceed their primary market dominating position.

Step Four - Determine your secondary market dominating position. What additional competitive advantages does your business offer that your customers will perceive as being different from your competition? Domino's secondary benefits included special pricing, assorted sizes, and a broader selection of toppings and additional menu items. What else can you offer to fortify your secondary market dominating position?

Step Five - Create your market dominating position statement and make it a part of your elevator pitch. This is a simple statement you create by combining Steps one through four. This helps you state unequivocally what differentiates you from your competitors to your targeted prospects and customers. Domino's market dominating position was neatly summed up in its slogan. "Fresh hot pizza delivered in 30 minutes or less or it's free." An expanded version of this could be, "Domino's provides busy customers with fresh, hot pizza within 30 minutes or less. Our assorted pizza offerings combined with our value pricing makes Domino's affordable to everyone."

Now, let's explore categories that set can your business apart from your competition.

Categories that Separate Your Business from Your Competition: Convenience

There are three categories that will enable you to separate your business from your competition. After reviewing them, you should be able to see which one best fits your individual business. Category one involves the level of service you provide for

Convenience. There are six different areas where you can "add value" when it comes to service. In today's hectic world, the one thing most people value more than money is more time. You can see this in the dramatic increase of convenience stores that typically charge 40% more for their products and services than traditional stores.

Their "get people in and out fast" is a market winning strategy. Few people have their oil changed at dealerships because local neighborhood oil change specialty shops are more convenient. The exponential growth of these shops is a direct result of people rejecting the inconvenience of dropping off their cars at the dealership; securing a ride home and then picking up their cars after having them serviced. The allure of the local oil change shop is based on convenience. Anything you do in your business to increase your customer convenience will create a market dominating advantage.

Next, we will explore six area to help you improve convenience for your customers can set you apart in the marketplace.

Six Areas To Improve Convenience

There are six areas to consider where you can provide your clients more convenience. The first area is **Location**. Although this may be one of the best ways to provide convenience, for the vast majority of businesses, changing locations is probably not an option. But make no mistake; being in a great location is surely a secondary market dominating position. For example, a fitness center located near an upscale residential area, location is a primary market dominating position.

If you have an online business, your website or platform must be user friendly. The download speed, the page layouts, and the mobile readiness must be able to keep up with the online demand to offer client convenience. Potential customers will navigate away and visit other sites that have these things in place and for you it could mean lost business.

The second area of convenience is **Availability**. Your customers want to do business when it is convenient for them. In other words, their schedule is the priority; not yours. Explore what you can do to make your business more available to your clients. Consider extending your hours and days you open for business.

For example, ten years ago most health clubs opened from 8 am through 7pm, Monday through Saturday. Today, the vast majority are open twenty-four hours, seven days a week. The clubs that resisted this open schedule struggled to survive and either had to close their doors or meet the needs of the changing market. Competition in this arena is tough and if anyone refuses to change, then their business suffers.

The same is true for supermarkets and convenience stores. We shop when we have time, not when the store thinks it's convenient for us to shop. This is the reason that is today's market, so many retail stores stay open twenty four hours a day. It's just good for business. It's also good for customers. In this super charged competitive and digital age, having an online shopping option makes things even more convenient for customers.

These points are just suggestions and you may not need to make changes. You are the only one who can determine whether your business needs to modify your hours to accommodate your customers. If you are not sure, try testing different operating hours to see what financially works best for your business. You can also do a customer survey. When customers give feedback, they not only give you answers but also suggestions on how to better serve them.

If you happen to be a financial planner, how would changing your hours to include some weekend or evenings help your clients who work Monday through Friday week? If your customers need to drop off items to you, then consider offering a drop box service. How long would customers patronize businesses like video stores, rental car companies, dry cleaners or shipping and auto body shops stay in business? These businesses know and understand the needs of their idea customers and having drop box service is not just an option. It's a convenient necessity for good business.

The third is **Ordering Process**. Ordering must be easy. If ordering is a headache for your customers, then it will impact your bottom line. Ensuring that your ordering process is easy helps you to establish a powerful market dominating position. Customers want what they want and want to go through the least amount of effort to get it. If the process proves to be laborious, then you can lose the sale.

Have you ever called a business and tried to speak with a real human being? The answering service looped you through a maze of automated voice mail messages asking you to select options that have nothing to do with your reason for calling. This is not only frustrating but it creates enough emotional animosity to compel a customer to take their business to a competitor. In contrast, the business that makes the ordering process convenient by providing easy access to menus with a live operator option or the ability to order online becomes the most logical customer choice.

A fourth area is **Delivery**. When a convenient location is not an option for your business, then offer the next best thing; bring your product or service to your customer! Businesses are sprouting up that specialize in delivering local restaurant items directly to your home or office. You call an 800 number and place your order from one of their listed, local area restaurants. The service then delivers the meal and charges a set fee that is typically 50% to 100% higher than visiting the restaurant in person.

The fact is people consider convenience more valuable than money. Even businesses like dry cleaners now use delivery to increase their revenue and profits. And to add a value, many of these cleaners also schedule home delivery and pick up. What more convenience can you ask for?

Another fast growing business segment is mobile services. This is where the business comes directly to your location to perform their services. A great example is a home decorator who offers shop-at-home service. The decorator brings swatches and samples to the customer's home and does a consultation by helping the customer select items that compliment their home and lifestyle. This personalized approach often leads to dramatic increases in conversion rates and takes price out of the equation.

On any given day you can see ads for window replacement services for your car. The technician comes directly to your location and replaces your window instead of you having to bring the vehicle to their shop. Commodity businesses like these should make mobile services a necessary part of their business model if possible. If you have a business like this, adding convenience easily positions your business as the logical choice.

The fifth area is **Payment Terms**. If your competition doesn't offer financing options, you can differentiate your business by offering payment terms over 30, 60, or 90 days. Offer multiple payment options such as a three easy payment plan or something similar. Did you know that a product or service that typically sells for 39.95 can be sold for twice that price by offering the customer a two payment option where they pay $39.95 at the time they place the order, and then an additional 39.95 in 30 days? Although this is a 100% increase in price, it only decreased the orders by less than 17% versus offering the product at the original 39.95 price point.

You can also consider accepting credit cards if you do not already accept them. This alone can increase your sales by as much as 80%. How would you feel if you had to pay cash every time you filled up your car or had to make an emergency run to the store? Think about it. It just makes sense, especially in today's market to accept credit cards.

The sixth and final area is **Miscellaneous Services**. What additional services do your customers consider to be important? If your business attracts parents with small children, consider offering child care services while the parents shop or takes care of business. What type of value would it be if restaurants offered quality, onsite child care? How would that service impact parents who would normally have to bring their children with them to dine out?

What is the value of having your children in the same location knowing they are being cared for while you dine? Do you believe parents could put a price on experiencing a quiet hour to have an enjoyable child free, worry free meal where they could actually check on their children if they wanted? What about the local bank? How often do busy parents have to bring their children to the bank and spend their entire time trying to quiet them instead of focusing on their banking?

If your business requires parents to evaluate their purchase decision, such as when buying furniture, a new computer or clothing, then it may be good to have a play area for their children. If your business requires lengthy transaction times or office visits, such as a dentist, doctor or health club, then having a child's play area can be a huge area of differentiation. So consider these six areas when looking for ways your business can provide more convenience.

Other Examples of Convenience Factors in Service

Speed is another area where you can add value. In today's fast paced society, speed and convenience are becoming major players in our customer's buying decisions. Find opportunities to add speed and your business can quickly dominate your market. If you think about it, both you and your customers like fast service.

When someone buys a home, they want a fast loan approval. Most mortgage brokers take weeks to make a decision. If you offer a product and you can deliver it within 48 hours, then you can easily be in a market dominating position. If you are a retailer, an express lane at your checkout counters is a major benefit to select customers, especially those who only need to purchase a few items. Grocery stores, airlines, rent-a-car companies and other businesses that offer frequent purchase benefits find express checkout to be a major incentive to prospects who value speed.

Education and training also adds value to your service. Prospects and customers today value education and training as much as they value price. They want to experience all the benefits your product or service offers them and they know that education and training can help them accomplish that goal. Entrepreneurs and business owners can instantly compete against major corporations by offering special and targeted training to their customers particularly when the major corporation fails to provide it. This is especially true if you are selling a commodity type of product or service where application knowledge is required.

Home Depot created a market dominating position by hiring former contractors and tradesmen to provide professional advice, tips and tricks in building and remodeling. They give detailed advice on the best way to complete home improvement projects. They also teach classes on various different building skills for their do-it-yourself customers. If you are a novice and you need guidance on your next remodeling project, then Home Depot is the logical choice.

Let's think about the holidays; more specifically Christmas. When was the last time you bought anything that said no assembly required? It seems as though every product we purchase these days requires us to assemble it or download something into it. Your computer, your child's bike or swing set, your backyard barbecue grill and of course, your iPhone. Look at the number of apps offered for downloading today. The instructions that accompany these items are usually terrible and should be labeled as impossible to interpret. In fact, by the time you actually assemble the item or download the software, you are so frustrated that you vow never to buy the product again. But what if easy step by step instructional videos that described each step of assembly in vivid, easy to follow detail or offered you a toll free number to call for immediate assistance accompanied these products? Think about the ease of use and the reduction of frustration.

It used to be that when your computer went on the fritz you were forced to log it to the nearest computer service center where it sat for weeks before the technician could get to it. Now you can download software in less than one minute that allows them to fully access your computer from their office, doing an instant analysis of what is wrong and usually repair it on the spot. By educating their clients that they provide this service and their competitors do not is enough to give them a major market dominating position. This doesn't just apply to product providers. Service providers can apply this same strategy to not only attract new clients to their business, but to help reduce their annual attrition rate.

An accountant, a CPA or bookkeeper or financial planner could offer to educate their clients on their numbers every month. Instead of giving their clients monthly statements (which 95% of business owners don't have time to view) these professionals can visit their client's offices and help set up their accounting and bookkeeping system. During this visit, they can answer any questions or address concerns in person. The bonus is that this is a free service to their clients. This type of service can result in a huge influx of new clients and in upwards of a 50% reduction in client attrition rates. It can help any organization review their pricing with value added differentials.

To emphasize this point, let's look at the financial impact this created for our client partner accountant firm Human Resources Partners Inc. in Cary, North Carolina. The owner Lori King had been in business for more than 15 years when we met. After an hour long interview, we knew we could work with her and also add value to her business. Most of her competitors offered the same 1 hour free assessment to clients but Lori wanted to add value and decided to offer an educational bonus to differentiate her business.

This strategy helped her clients to see their business health in a different way. This educational bonus helped to create a more transparent view of her clients' business health. Instead of having a compliance based mind set and gathering end of year receipts and handing them over to an accountant, Lori helped them to see the actual "money flow" of their business.

This bonus helped them create a more financially robust enterprise because they learned to look at the numbers as part of business health. Because Lori added value through educating her clients, this strategy paid off not only in building a strong bond of client trust, but she was also able to move her pricing from $90/hour to $95/hour.

This is just a slight 5% increase and we believe she can do more with the extraordinary added value she now offers her clients. Let's assume that the typical accountant averages 250 clients. If each client takes 5 hours/month, that is an increase of $75,000 in additional income each year. People tend to stay longer with an accountant they like because of the confidential nature of the profession. With an average client lifetime of 5 years, this is an increase of $375,000 over 5 years. Also remember that as the firm continues the education program, their individual client pricing can increase. We are not counting in the new referrals coming in from satisfied clients. At this writing, she presently now charges $99/hour!

Can the business still lose clients? Of course, but the accounting firm is still better off providing the educational differential for their clients. What about their attrition rate? The impact is not only financial but it also helped Lori filter her clients' database to work with her ideal clients. But, there is still more. She now has the opportunity to serve even more of her clients in this process. Since the education is a consistent part of her business, how difficult would it be for her to incorporate presenting her clients with additional areas where she can help in adding value? Since her firm is now a trusted member of her clients' business team, she can help them expand their product or service offering through joint ventures or strategic partnership endorsements.

We have to clarify and disclaim here that at this writing, our accountant has no commissions on referral respecting her core values. These clients of our accountant would gladly pay the accountant to help them execute these new strategies. This could easily add an additional income and profit to this accountant's bottom line. Even if 50% of the average original two hundred fifty clients participated in this offer annually, that represents one hundred twenty-five clients. By losing half of their client base, the firm will still be better off and target their ideal clients with peace of mind in their practice than having the stress of work with difficult clients. After all this, and we still did not factor in new referrals to the accountant coming in from satisfied clients.

If your business involves a particular level of technical expertise or the application of individual skills, this is a powerful value added service. This could easily apply to a printer that provides graphic designs and copy expertise, a lone maintenance contractor that specializes in botanical gardens or a business that employs Spanish speaking staff in an area with a high concentration of non-English speaking Hispanics. This implies that your business provides targeted expertise and you simply need to inform your target market that you have it.

Another area where you can add value is to completely remove all potential purchase risk to the prospect. A 100% money back guarantee or generous return policies are quickly becoming the norm in most industries. However, look at your industry closely and if you find that none of your competitors offer 100% money back guarantee, then you have the opportunity to make your business the only logical choice by doing so.

For example, major retailer Nordstrom's created a world class reputation around their no-questions-asked guarantee. Knowing that you can take anything back for any reason at any time if you are not completely satisfied eliminates any risk of purchase. Why would anybody purchase the same item at the same price from any other store? It's important to note that your return rate represents a scientifically calculated risk for your business. Return rates have become a constant over time and will seldom vary by more than a few percentage points one way or the other. This ensures you will know your exact cost when offering your guarantee.

The fifth area of service is quality. Although quality is a vague term, it is powerful when it comes to setting your business apart from others. Think of quality as the perceived benefit received by the customer. Papa John's Pizza's market dominating position is substantially different from Domino's. Domino's focus was on hungry college students that wanted pizza fast and cheap. They focused on providing low cost pizza for an affordable price. Papa John's focused their marketing on stating that they on provided only the finest ingredients and a special recipe crust with slightly higher pricing. Both businesses used the exact same methods for making a pizza but Papa John's carved out a targeted niche that made them the logical choice for people seeking what they believed was better quality pizza.

The sixth and final additional area where you can add value is security and safety. With internet scams and online fraud making daily headlines and overall crime rates at an all time high, security and safety have now entered the decision making process for most prospects when it comes to purchase selection.

If your business is located in a less desirable neighborhood or you serve children or the elderly, ask yourself what steps can you take to make your prospects feel totally safe? A store in a less desirable part of town could hire a security guard or provide access to a secure parking lot. These additions can differentiate you from your competitors who offer no additional security services. A building contractor could leverage tremendously on this area to differentiate themselves.

Be sure you consider these six areas of service as a way to add massive value and create a market dominating position for your business. Only you know your business and what you want to accomplish. It never hurts to have some assistance in developing strategies that help you reach your business goals. Contact us to see how we can help! Now, let's explore how to separate your business from your competition.

Categories To Separate Your Business
From Your Competition

Back in its heyday, Blockbuster dominated the video market by stocking more hit movies than its smaller competitors. A larger selection of movies and inventory of new releases meant a customer had a much better chance of finding their desired movie at Blockbuster than they did at their local video store. Blockbuster created a market dominating position where they guaranteed the new release would be available whenever their customers wanted to rent. Unfortunately for Blockbuster, the convenience factor we discussed earlier quickly came into play. Never forget that convenience is the primary consideration for most prospects.

In Blockbuster's case, it simply was not convenient to constantly make trips back and forth to their local stores to pick up and return movies. Netflix, however duplicated the Blockbuster model by selection and then added the convenience of never having to leave your home to rent a movie. The results speak for themselves. Blockbuster went from $6.1 billion in total revenue in 2004 to bankruptcy in 2010, while Netflix went from $506 million to $2.2 billion in revenue in that same time frame and it's still going strong.

In the case of Netflix, all they had to do was match their competition in the area of selection and innovate in the area of convenience. Selection can include different models, shapes, sizes, styles, colors and so on. Just look at the computer, mobile phone or PDA markets. For years you only had a single color choice. Now you have your choice of multiple colors and prospects are responding, especially teenagers.

If you are a retailer, offering a greater selection may be as simple as combining different products or services to create a bundle offer. What combination of products and services will appeal to your various customer groups? Jos. A Bank specializes in men's apparel. They are masters and often bundle packages to increase their customer purchase amounts. Television ads proclaim customers can buy one of their suits at regular price and receive a second suit and three dress shirts free of charge. Since they offer a huge selection of styles and colors, this promotion always gets a big response.

Categories To Separate Your Business From Your Competition

The third and final category is pricing. If price represents your market dominating position, you are selling for low profit margins at best. Never forget that prospects buy value, not price. If you fail to convince a prospect about your value, you can cut your price in half and you still will not get the sale. However, if you combine price with other market dominating advantages, then price can be a compelling tool.

Price differentiates your business in three ways. The first example is do you want single or fixed pricing? Businesses that differentiate themselves by offering a set price are those that charge by the hour, the unit, the number of services they provide, the amount of food eaten or the number of products used. All amusement parks used to charge for individual rides. Now they charge a general admission fee with unlimited rides. Bowling alleys now offer unlimited bowling for a fixed fee. Place like Ryan's, Golden Corral, and Home Town Buffet continue to offer all-you-can-eat meals for around $10. Fixed pricing can still be used for most businesses to establish the market dominating position, especially when you use a little imagination.

A great example is an attorney could charge a flat fee to handle traffic violations, court appearances, as well as divorces. A pest control company could charge a set annual fee where they agree to exterminate your home every three months and provide unlimited service calls if the pests return. A golf course could partner with other local courses and they could all agree to sell memberships at a fixed price that gives unlimited access to all the courses for the year.

You can also use fixed pricing on a per visit or per session basis. For example, a tanning salon could offer unlimited tanning sessions during the summer months. A movie theater could offer unlimited admission to all shows with the purchase of a day pass. This offer would be good on their slowest day of the week as a way to increase attendance as well as revenue.

The second way price differentiates your business is by increasing or decreasing your prices. Prospects often judge the quality of your product or service by the price you charge. A price that they perceive to be extremely low instantly sends off warning bells in their decision making process that this must not be a high quality product or service. Believe it or not, businesses can actually raise their pricing and instantly reposition their product or service to give it the perception of being the superior choice without changing anything else.

This is especially true on products and services that we know very little about. Gold is often considered a lucrative investment and yet we guarantee that if we run an ad offering a one ounce Krugerrand gold coin worth $2000 for $20 dollars, we would not receive so much as one serious inquiry. No one would think that ad was serious based on the price alone, even if we just happened to be an eccentric millionaire looking to make the world a better place.

For most prospects, price indicates quality. Take wine as a primary example. Someone buying wine as a gift may assume the more expensive wine must be better and yet taste is not exactly an exact science. Much of what we taste is in our heads and not in the wine. One of the most powerful elements in wine tasting is temperature. Wine is perception in its profound experience. It is something to share and discover with loved ones. Yet most people would be ashamed to bring their host a $6 bottle of wine versus a $50 bottle even when the $6 bottle tastes as good or better. In fact, when it comes to most of the products and services we purchase, we gladly pay more for name brands versus the generic versions. This same branding made diamonds dominate the world of romance and relationships.

Cheerios is one of the top selling breakfast cereals in the world. It is made from whole grain oats and sells for close to $4 per box and yet every grocery store on the planet offers their own store version of this cereal that is identical to Cheerios for less than half the price. Consider testing specific items or service packages to see if it works for your business. For example, if you are a business coach, you may be perceived as more valuable if you charge $250 per hour instead of your standard $125. This can be validated quickly by testing the price changing, engaging the prospects' reaction. You can also always down sell them to the lower price if necessary.

The third way price differentiates your business is by offering small value added services. There are always customers who will gladly

pay you a little extra to receive a higher level of service. If you believe this applies to your business, you may want to think about raising your service level along with your pricing. Consider the airlines today. They now charge for everything from baggage fees, pillows, blankets and even beverages. Southwest Airlines, however, still provides all these services complimentary. They even allow you to check two bags free of charge. All this added value and yet they still consistently offer the lowest price in the airline industry. They are also the only airline who has made a quarterly profit every quarter except for one in the last 40 years.

The Power of Value added Services: Million Dollar Business

Value added service doesn't require you to make huge investments to execute the strategy. It's often little things that make the biggest difference. Just training your staff to pleasantly greet your customers and calling them by their name may make all the difference in the world. Offer your customers a complimentary cup of coffee or bring in bagels once a week on your busiest day. Find a way to give your customers something they value. As you can see, convenience, selection and price make up the three categories that will enable you to separate your business from your competition. Use the examples we have provided to help you find your own market dominating position for your business. Once you do, you can create your million dollar business.

Value strengthens your powerful and compelling elevator pitch, which is the way you want to communicate your market dominating position to your target customers. To create this message effectively, contact our office for assistance. We can equip you to create, design and develop your very own multi-million dollar business. As you can see, our overall focus is to help you build the business you've always dreamed of owning; a business that provides you with financial freedom and an extraordinary life for you and your family. Now, let's explore a client case study that demonstrates what we have been covering.

Case Study on Strategic Positioning

Here's an additional example to illustrate the power of the market dominating position. One of our previous clients was a roofing contractor with a well-known national roofing shingles and materials. We will use the name MBE Materials, Inc. At that time, he specialized in offering residential roof replacement with a free roof assessment. He professionally repaired or replaced roofs so houses looked almost new. After several successful years replacing roofs, he needed to give his business a new direction. Talking about convenience, we noticed that his prospects and customers were trending away from just roof replacement and looking for offers that will make their decision process easier.

We decided it was time to make some changes to his business. We conducted a survey of his previous customer base to discover exactly what it was they wanted when replacing the roofs for their homes. Number one on this list was personalized service. Most people know absolutely nothing about roof materials, quality, durability and resistance to the wind. They wanted a professional who could take them by the hand and help them make a wise decision that matched their lifestyle. They wanted a customized solution and they preferred a shop at home option so they could compare each materials sample to their home's outlook, their present décor and match it against their environments.

We also obtained some typical survey responses such as large selection, low price, extended warranty, free cleaning, and discounted accessories to include shingles. We equipped our client to find his strategic position which he now identified as frustrated homeowners that demand personal in-home service. His primary market dominating position became customized roofing services from the comfort of your home. His secondary market dominating position focused on offering a large selection of shingles, extended warranty, free cleaning, and discounts on accessories. Once he had this clearly defined, he could now create his supporting business model to make sure he could deliver on his implied promises and positioning.

We trained him and his team to sell based on the value offered. We recommended taking a few additional small samples of the most requested styles and colors to his prospects. He started carrying a more diversified selection of small samples, each of them segmented by style, color and quality variation. That alone greatly increased their conversion rates since most prospects are in their peak buying state when they are most excited when making choices. We also made an additional business change of targeting commercial roofing and multi-family roofing that should make a significant impact on conversion.

Although tape measures are an accurate way to measure things around the house, the customers seemed worried about his manual measurements. They became especially concerned when they were unable to directly see the actual measurements for themselves. To alleviate this concern, we advised our client to add a laser measurement system to his supporting business.

You can now purchase inexpensive laser devices that measure room sizes to the millimeter and then display the results digitally for everyone to see. This immediately established trust with the prospects who knew for sure they were being charged for the exact number of shingles or roofing materials they needed. With all these components in place, he brought and created his primary market dominating position as well as a second one.

Market Differentiation Categories Review

Let's quickly review the six categories that help you differentiate your business from your competition. Here again are the six categories:

- Location
- Availability
- Ordering Process
- Payment Terms
- Miscellaneous Services
- Quality
- Security & Safety

Do not forget the value and impact of adding an educational and training component to your business. Remember, your most valuable asset is you and the information and service you provide!

How to Strategically Position Your Business

Now that you have some fresh ideas to consider, let's look at some examples that show you how to properly identify and position your strategic position, primary market dominating position, secondary market dominating position with supporting business model.
Let's begin again with an accountant. Let's assume that this accountant has a passion for helping new small business owners. Their strategic position would be small business start-ups. Their primary market dominating position could include consulting with

new business owner regarding the best financing options or the proper corporate structure to minimize their tax liability. Another option may include guiding them in office equipment and computer system selection to minimize tax burden.

A third option may include helping them to initially set up their book keeping and accounting system at no charge. Their secondary market dominating position might include a free consultation and access to the accountant's proprietary software programs. Whatever they select as their primary and secondary market dominating positions, they must build a supporting business model to deliver on their promise. They may appoint a dedicated staff member that has small business expertise and in-depth knowledge when it comes to small business loans, funding, investors, or strategic alliances with other experts in any or all these areas.

Their staff may need specialized training in small business management or start-ups. It may require programs and services outsourcing and initially providing the training free of charge to reduce the financial exposure to this accountant. Once all these are clearly and specifically identified, the accountant can then use these four areas to create their very own market dominating message or statement.

Again, let's look at the roofing contractor who specializes in unique materials and replacement projects. Their strategic position would be unique, one of kind roof replacement projects for upscale homes. In this specific situation unique, one of a kind roof replacement projects can also be their primary market dominating position. They may choose to emphasize the fact that they have an entire network of custom building specialists on staff. They can also offer a no cost, no obligation initial assessment with recommendations for their homeowners. Another possibility is they may maintain a staff of on-site shingles technicians. All these would be excellent primary market dominating positions.

Another facet of their market dominating position could include having all subcontractors sign a code of ethics that requires specific behaviors on the job in the event the homeowners may have small children. They should also sign a lien waiver agreeing not to place a lien on the homeowner's property. These two facets provide a blanket of safety for homeowners and shows your concern for the safety and security of their home and privacy.

Other secondary market dominating positions might include a monthly, quarterly or yearly cleaning crew who leaves their homeowners roofs spotless. It would serve as a part of a prevention program of early damages to the roof. With the changing climate bringing hurricanes and also with changes in seasons, it will help homeowners feel more secure to know they have an eye on their roofs. Whatever they select to be their primary and secondary market dominating positions, they need a strong supporting business model to deliver on their promise.

Have an attorney create a formal lien waver form for signing along with a code of conduct and ethics standard template. This contractor may need to hire custom craftsmen to specialize in specific personalized projects such as GAF shingles and materials installation expertise, access to custom order materials and services as well as custom tools and equipment to create unique features and experience for the homeowner within these high dollar homes. Once everything is clearly and specifically identified, the roofing contractor can use these four areas to create their own market dominating message or statement.

Use these examples to guide you in identifying your strategic position along with your market dominating position. Build your business model so you can easily and consistently deliver on your market dominating position and then create your market dominating statement so that when every qualified prospect hears it, it immediately feels as though they would be missing out if they bought from anyone but you.

SECTION TWO

Target Customers' Physical Profile: Demographics

"If there was any doubt on the part of our male colleagues about women's ability during the early part of our struggle, it proved baseless." - Paul Kagame, President of Rwanda

SECTION TWO

Target Customers' Physical Profile: Demographics

Every entrepreneur, business owner or start up wants to build a successful and lucrative business. This chapter will help you begin that process and develop a critically important component that directly impacts the ultimate success of your business. You must be able to clearly identify your target customer. Here is an example to illustrate the importance of knowing, understanding and identifying your target customer.

A US based pharmacy chain conducted a testing in four markets of a new customer rewards program called Wellness+. For their national rollout, they posted promises on the company website. The card offered free sign-up and customers could earn points to earn discounts on pharmacy brand products. Customers could also receive coupons in the mail. They also offered an additional new benefit of earning points towards free healthcare screenings.

Here's the challenge. When a card holder received five hundred points or spent $500 on non-prescription products (one point is worth $1), they received a certificate they could use for free health screenings, like glucose and cholesterol readings. The program also gave twenty-five points for each prescription filled but did not include prescriptions paid for in whole or in part by state or federal healthcare programs like Medicare or Medicaid.

But isn't it safe to assume that people who spent $50 at the pharmacy or filled twenty prescriptions at the counter were already screened? Who was the company actually targeting? The American healthcare system is in disarray and pharmacies like Walgreens have stepped up to fill the affordable healthcare void with inexpensive healthcare screenings and advice. So, what was this pharmacy thinking?

Shouldn't first-step screening that are so vital and important to customer health come more often than when a customer spends $500 on products like toilet paper and a KitKat bar? Rewards for more affluent customers who can afford to spend $500 on non-prescription items, or are constantly filling prescriptions at the store, didn't seem to be the best way to promote public health.

Real innovation would be free screenings for poverty line customers, or establishing a more realistic point offering. This was a classic case of putting the cart before the horse, as the old adage says. This major retailer failed miserably to even remotely analyze who their target customer is and what they want. There is no magic to selling. A business must discover what their customers want and then give it to them. The pharmacy chain completely missed the boat with this program.

Two critical fundamentals are understanding and knowing your target customer and then mapping out their thought process for innovation. Once you can execute your plan in order to build a successful and profitable business. The next step is creating a customer's physical profile.

Customer's Physical Profile Overview

Whatever you do in business, defining your perfect target market is critical. To begin, let's focus on four major components specifically designed to help you find your target customers. The first step is identifying their physical characteristics, which is often referred to as a demographic profile. It is imperative that you have a clear mental picture of the physical attributes of your target customers.

In the future, this information will help you pinpoint your target customer once you begin marketing to them. This will make it easier to find them and get your marketing message in front of them. Let's explore why it's so important for your business to clearly identify your target customer and how it will help you build the business you've always dreamed of having.

Your target customer is one who shares the purpose and passion for your products or services. These are customers who want what you offer as opposed to just needing what you offer. They don't just use what you offer; they love it. They not only purchase what you sell; they actually feel they couldn't live without it.

Connecting with your target customer will result in fewer returns and complaints. These customers are thrilled with you and your business. They buy from you today and they keep buying from you until a competitor understands them better than you do. They put a demand on you to create additional products and services because they trust you and they know you have their best interest at heart. They tell their circle all about you and encourage them to do business with you. And best of all, they spend more money with you over their lifetime than your average customer. Your target customers provide your business with tons of referrals and offer you unsolicited testimonials. They also praise you and your business on social networking sites and garners you free publicity.

When you identify your target customer, you will find yourself loving what you do and moving forward in your purpose. The end result is that you work less and earn more; a lot more! This impacts your business long-term. It impacts all future products and services you develop. It impacts your customer service to your clients and it impacts all your marketing and sales efforts. It also especially helps when you develop your marketing materials and sales scripts. Knowing and understanding your target customer's identity plays a vital role in building a successful business. Here is an additional component your target customer provides that can make you wealthy without doing anything more than what you're already doing.

You're probably familiar with the 80/20 principle. Simply put, it says that small focused actions lead to big results. For example, count the number of clothes you have hanging in your closet. Next, count the pieces of clothing you frequently wear. You will discover that you wear about 20% of your clothes 80% of the time. Your business functions in much the same way. Approximately 20% of your customers account for about 80% of your business revenue. That 20% of your customers are your target customers. Just imagine the possibilities for your business if you could attract more customers like them. But wait; what would your business look like if you could alter that ratio and attract 40% of your target customers instead of 20%? That means your revenue doubles. Do you now see the impact of identifying your target customers and how it can have a dramatic impact on your business?

This information is so critical that if you attract 100% of your target customers, your revenue would explode by a factor of 16. If you're making $2,000 per month right now, just replacing your current customers with target customers will increase your monthly revenue to $32,000. And best of all, these target customers don't require you to generate any additional time, effort or energy. This is an example of how you can work smarter and not harder. This is how you make more money while working fewer hours, and it all starts by clearly identifying your target customer. That's the power of the 80/20 principle. Unfortunately, most startups, entrepreneurs and business owners are only attracting about 20% of their target customers, even though these are the most profitable customers in their businesses.

So, how do you attract target customers? You must have the proper fundamentals in place to make this work. After you identify them, you will be able to identify what they want. If you discover that your business doesn't offer what they want or if you offer a solution but it's the exact same solution as your competitors offer, then you must become innovative. You can then offer your customers the most value when compared to your competition. Once you do this, you will explode your revenue and profits to new heights without adding any additional time or effort. But here's the really exciting part of the 80/20 principle. To get 16 times better results than what you're getting right now, you don't have to do anything different than what you're already doing.

All you have to do is more of what you're already doing that's working well. Figure out why the current 20% of your target customers are buying from you and start attracting more of them by creating and developing compelling marketing. This is the solution. Most entrepreneurs, business owners and startups struggle with creating compelling marketing. That's okay because you don't know what you don't know. Understanding your customers on a continuous basis is not a trivial matter. Continue reading because we're going to reveal marketing secrets used by the pros and in the process, position you and your business as the only logical buying choice for your customers

First, we need to help you develop your target customer's physical profile by completing a detailed physical characteristic analysis. Remember, we want to start by identifying everyone on the planet who needs what you sell. We're going to help you develop this vital information by going to the appendix and using the target customer profile form.

Later on in section 3, we'll focus on helping you develop the emotional profile for your target customer. The emotional profile defines your target customer's emotional switches, situations, worries and concerns. We need to know specifically what they really want from your product or service. The emotional profile helps you define what your ideal clients want and not need. Once developed, it perfectly complements the physical profile and forms a crystal clear picture of your perfect target customer. So, let's first define the available universe of human beings that need what you sell. We'll discover that with the physical profile.

Assignment on Customers' Physical Profile

You may noticed, each section in this book builds on the previous section, so you can take your time and complete each assignment. Your present assignment is an important one and will prepare you for more extensive content we'll cover. So, let's begin to define the general physical profile of your target customer.

Remember that the physical profile defines the available universe of every human being on the planet that needs what you sell. We want you to create a list of traits that you believe defines that universe as it applies to your business, and record those traits using the forms at the end of the section.

Again, you can also access the digital forms at the link mentioned at the end of the section. You only need to fill in the top center box for now. We will complete this form during the progress through the 5 steps. So be sure you keep this form in a safe place. Keep in mind that when listing these traits, we are not talking about the clients who want what you sell. Focus first on those who need what you sell. We have covered several completed examples for your review if you need to go back and read.

Please use the indicated forms at the end of the section to verify that the traits you've listed are the right traits for your business. For example, if you sell business-to-business services, use the form labeled B2B. If you sell to consumers, use the form labeled B2C. Use these to record the actual physical profiles for the consumers or businesses you're profiling.

We recommend that you use this process. Begin by researching six current customers, if you have current customers. If you're a start-up, you may not have any customers at this time. If you don't have current customers, don't worry about it and ask close friends or friends of friends. Just ask yourself, who on the face of this planet may at some point in their life need what you sell. This isn't rocket science so don't make this hard on yourself. This is simply your starting point.

Let's first consider age ranges and select the youngest mid-range and oldest male and female customers you currently serve. You don't need to physically interview them. Just record the information you know about them. It's okay to guess if you don't know for sure. You're just establishing the basic ranges for now. In other words, It won't matter if someone is 56 years-old and you write down 60. Do the same thing when it comes to determining income level. Most people will be offended if you ask them how much they make. But, if you know their current profession, you can make an educated guess as to the approximate income level. You might also look online for average income ranges for that specific profession depending upon your country data available.

Another way to gather information is to capture their zip code since most zip codes are an excellent indicator of specific income levels in some countries. Once you record this information using the age ranges for both your male and female clients, repeat this process as it applies to marital status. Again, choose current customers that represent the youngest, mid-range, and oldest single, married and divorced customers you presently serve. This should get you started in developing a fairly accurate information range. You can revise this general list later and make it much more specific and refined.

When you complete your research, use the forms on summary in the end of the section. Summarize the research you perform and record it for easy reference. In the event you sell business-to-business, use the related summary form to record the physical profile information for the businesses you sell to. Again, it's labeled B2B for easy reference. Begin by choosing three current business customers that sell a product and three that sell a service. Then, look at their annual revenue and record the business with the lowest revenue, approximate mid-range revenue, and the highest revenue.

Finally, look over the number of people they employ and rank them from the lowest to the highest. You're only establishing general categories that form an overall summary of your current client business types.

If you are a massage therapist, you may be working with a business owner who is a solo professional who is an accountant and makes $50,000 annually with no employees, all the way up to a major corporation that hires you to come into their offices twice per month to provide chair massages to their executive team. They may employ 50 people and generate $50 - $100 million in revenue. That's the range you want to record. Use this form to summarize your data, but keep in mind that using your current clients is just a quick way to get started. We still want you to assess whether additional physical traits also apply. Remember, define the available universe of human beings or businesses that need what you sell. Use the current clients as a starting point but don't limit yourself to only their physical description.

The main reason we want you to begin with your current customers is profound. You must be presently doing something to attract these customers. This will come into play when you create your marketing program. This way, you will have that data available at your finger tips. By completing this exercise, you will begin the development of an accurate profile for your target customer. You'll be able to physically identify them when you see them and you'll know where to look for them when you start your marketing program. Just remember to use the forms in the end of the section or download a digital copy for your use.

Our next section, we will take a look at the emotional profile for your target customer. We will also explain why emotions are 90% of the small and medium sized business success journey. Things really get interesting during this phase because the emotional profile helps you discover your target customer's emotional switches or triggers. You discover the problems, frustrations, fears and con-cerns your target customers tend to share as a group. When you discover their emotional switches, they open the door for your busi-ness to dominate your market.

They can turn on your qualified prospects interests in what you sell. This is where it gets exciting, so start preparing yourself. This pro-cess depends on you doing a great job on this physical profile assignment. Our mission is to equip you to build the business of your dreams. Working together with your team, there's nothing to stop you from accomplishing that goal.

FORMS

Business 2 Business (B2B) PHYSICAL PROFILE

Name [   ] Title [   ]

Business Name [   ]

Adress [   ]

City [   ] State [   ] Zip [   ] Country [   ]

Email [   ] Phone [   ]

Website [   ]

Number Of Employees [   ]

Headquaters Location [   ]

Products/Services Type [   ]

Annual Revenue [   ]

Number of branches [   ]

Branches Location [   ]

Year founded [   ]

Organizational Structure [   ]

Title of Decision-Maker [   ]

Decision-Maker [   ]

Influencer [   ]

User [   ]

INSTRUCTIONS

1. Enter the results gathered from your physical profile

2. Where applicable, mention information as a range such as Number of Employees (5-10)

3. Highlight or mark similar items in each row, to identify trends that can help you better target your prospects

	Subject 1	Subject 2	Subject 3
Number of Employees			
Headquarters Location			
Products/Service Type			
Annual Revenue(Range)			
Number of Branches			
Branches Location			
Year Founded			
Organizational Structure			
Title of decision -maker			
Decision Maker			
Influencer			
User			

Business Name [   ]

Address [   ]

City [   ] State [   ] Zip code [   ] Country [   ]

Email [   ] Phone [   ]

Gender [   ]

Age [   ]

Marital Status [   ]

Yearly Income
(Dollars, Euros, Franc) [   ]

Education Level [   ]

Job Title/Profession [   ]

Typical Buying Patterns [   ]

Prior Purchase To Purchasing what you Sell [   ]

Related Products/Services Purchase [   ]

Notes [   ]

BUSINESS 2 CONSUMER (B2C)
Summary

Instructions
1. Enter the results gathered from your physical profile
2. In the summary analysis, summarize all three profiles to identify trends

	Subject 1	Subject 2	Subject 3
Gender			
Age			
Marital Status			
Yearly income (Dollars, Euro, Franc)			
Education Level			
Job Title/Profession			
Typical Buying Patterns			
Prior Purchase To Purchasing what u Sell			
Related Products/Services Purchase			

SUMMARY ANALYSIS

Gender	Male	Female	Male & Female	
Age				
Marital Status	Married	Single	Divorced	
Yearly Income (Dollars, Euros, Franc)				
Education Level	High School	BS/BA	Masters	PhD
Job Title/Profession				
Typical Buying Patterns				
Prior Purchase To Purchasing what u Sell				
Related Products/Services Purchase				

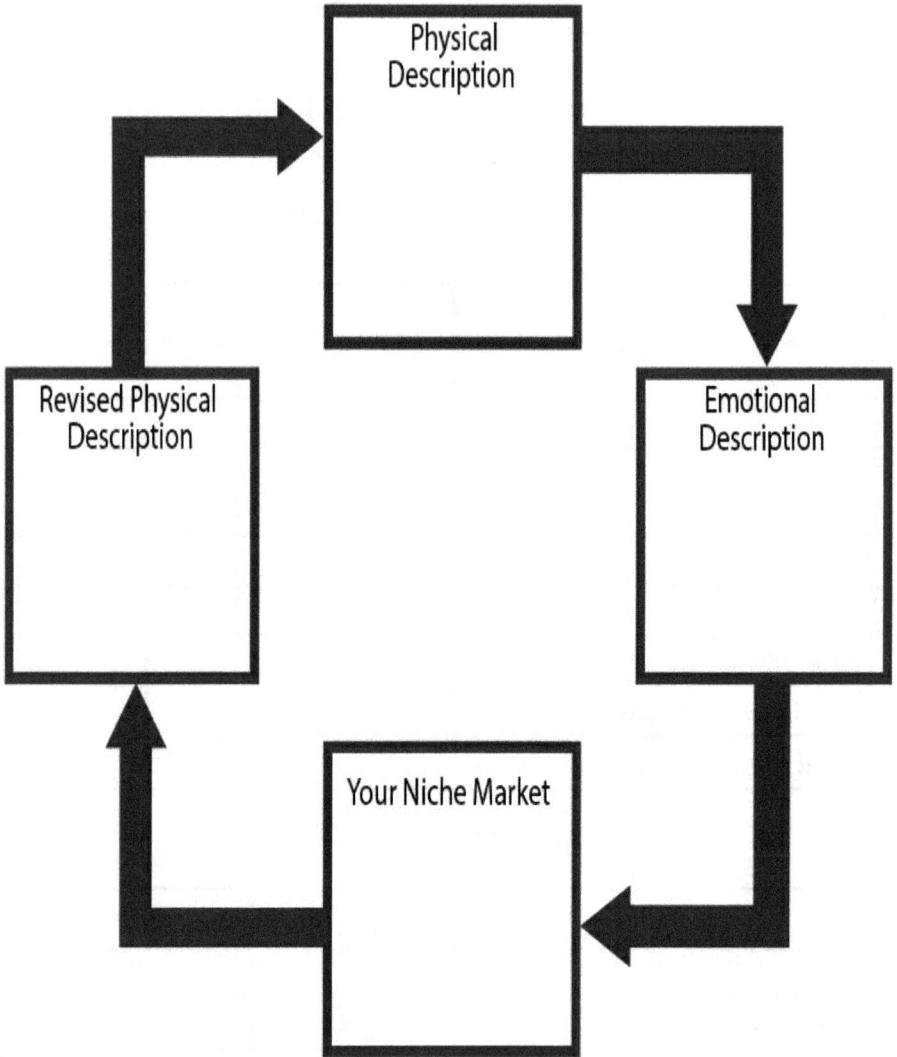

SECTION THREE
Target Customer Emotional Profile

"You don't judge someone drowning in a river when you didn't cross it yourself first." - African Proverb

SECTION THREE
Target Customer Emotional Profile: Psychographic

Now it's time to determine the emotional makeup or psychographics of your target customer. This is one of the most important of the five steps to help you gain market domination. Remember that prospects buy based on emotion and only use logic to justify their purchase. This is where you need to identify what we refer to as their emotional switches. They are the problems, fears, frustrations and concerns most prospects experience when they buy what you sell.

Going to the dentist makes most people think of pain. The thought of pain leads to fear. When you visit your doctor's office, the typically long waiting time can frustrate you. You're concerned when you go in for auto repairs because the final price usually doesn't match the estimate. If you can accurately identify your prospect's emotional triggers issues and then innovate your business to forever solve them, you create a market dominating position. You should also consider additional psychographic areas such as their health, their hobbies, interests, sports, education, personal causes, political and social, and leisure activities.

Let's continue developing your target customer profile. This is one of several critical business fundamentals and it impacts the ultimate success of your business. We previously discussed the importance of knowing and understanding your target customer's physical pro file. In this section, we'll discuss a far more important component in the target customer equation; the customer emotional profile. These emotional components define your target customer and help you to thoroughly understand what they want. Let's take a look at an example.

Example of Emotional Profiling

One of our previous clients is a photographer: Right Image Photography Inc. He had enjoyed a thriving business for many years, but he always thought his clients valued his photography because of his fast turn-around times, his low prices, and his technical expertise. One day, he did something that 99% of all entrepreneurs or business owners fail to do. He surveyed his target customers and asked why they did business with him.

When he completed interviewing several clients, he discovered that the benefits of low price and turn-around times were hardly ever mentioned by his customers. The number one thing they said they valued was his creativity. This illustration shows you why it's critical to understand what motivates your customers to buy; what it is they want and need, and then market to them based on those wants and needs.

Let's be honest. At various life stages, everyone needs a photographer. Parents want to capture their children's pictures for birthday and special celebrations. Since these parents need a special photographer, most of them shop around for a photographer that offers the lowest price. That's a typical first step of prospects that need a product or service. They are price shoppers, plain and simple.

So ask yourself; is that the market you want to serve? Are these the prospects that will satisfy the burning passion of your life's work? You have an enthusiasm of providing service to clients who care about your skill or expertise and those who appreciate the true value you provide. The above mentioned prospects are not your clients.

Fortunately for our photographer, he created value for a specific group of customers that wanted what he offered. In this case, they loved his creativity. His business attracted a special group of customers who wanted more than low prices and special deals. They wanted one-of-a-kind photographs that only a photographer with imagination and a willingness to throw caution to the wind was capable of producing.

To his select group of customers, price never entered into their decision. They valued what they wanted and they were willing to pay extra to get it. These customers can be identified by their emotional profile. So in this section, we'll focus on developing the emotional component of your target customer profile. As a reminder, we've included an end of the section with forms in this book. We want to reinforce the information we're covering and the ability to review this information at anytime in the future.

Customer's Emotional Profile

We've already outlined the basic components of the target customer profile. Let's briefly review why a target customer profile is so important for your business and how you can use it to build the business you've always wanted. This involves identifying the physical profile of all human beings on the planet who may have a need for what you sell, either now or sometime in the future. This is great information since you can use this information to locate your target customers when you begin to elaborate or improve your marketing program.

However, the simple truth is that the physical makeup of your target customer is responsible for about 10% of your business or entrepreneurial success journey. The reason for this low percentage is based on the way human beings make decisions. They buy based on their emotions. That means about 90% of your success will be determined by how accurately you define your target customer's emotional profile.

When you know and understand human emotions, you can predict, with greater accuracy, exactly what your target customers want. By developing an emotional profile, you reveal specifically what they want. This means that you can innovate your business to give them what they want. The emotional profile identifies the switches that "turns them on" emotionally. When your prospects purchase what you sell, feelings of frustration, fear and concern leave their minds.

The physical profile you completed earlier only defined the prospects that have a logical need to use your product or service. But the emotional profile defines the prospects that have an emotional reason to buy. In other words, they actually want what you sell. Your prospects are searching for solutions to what is troubling them emotionally. If you provide the solution they want, you offer the most value when they compare you to your competition. They will then buy from you every time.

Always remember that everyone wants the best deal and not necessarily the lowest price. It means the most value for the price they pay. Your prospects are willing to pay twice the price your competitors charge if you offer four times the value. It simply comes down to wants versus needs. When you need something, you make logical decisions. When you want something, you make emotional decisions. Think about it. Most people would love to own a Lamborghini. They sell for around $300,000. No one actually needs a Lamborghini but many people want one.

The formula for small business success is actually easy. Find the customers who want what you sell and position your compelling marketing message in front of them. Announce your solution while removing any risk for them to experience it for themselves. It is really just that straight forward.

Physical Profile Vs Emotional Profile

Here's a concern. If you try to describe the physical differences between the customers who need what you sell versus those who want what you sell, you would find it almost impossible to do. That's because both groups look the same physically. You previously identified the physical traits for your target customers. This profile only describes the physical components of the available universe of human beings who need what you sell. If you sell to consumers, you look at demographics, gender, age, marital status, and employment and income status. If you sell to other businesses, you look at annual revenue, location and the number of employees and corporate structure are important. These are physical components and the challenge is that physically, consumers and businesses look alike when you compare target customers with the general public.

So, how do we tell the difference? The real difference lies in knowing and understanding their emotional makeup. Entrepreneurs and business owners want to get their business in front of only those customers that want what they sell. They want those unique individuals who are emotionally drawn to their product or service. When you place their marketing message in front of these customers and give them a risk-free way experience of what you offer, make sure your product or service gives them a solution to their problem. Also make sure your solution offers the most value and you'll have a customer for life.

The key is to focus on what they want and evolve your products and services around their emotional profile. We've already said that when it comes to small and medium sized business success, the physical profile is responsible for about 10% of the success equation. The emotional profile accounts for about 90%. Right now, you may be thinking that this sounds like an impossible mission. But this is really a very simple process. But what's even better is that once you master this process, you'll be able to generate all the leads you want and attract as many clients as your business can handle. But like any process, there is step-by-step strategy you must follow.

We've already covered three steps for your market domination position. You've found your strategic position and defined your target market make ups. We've provided you with a profile summary form in the end of the section so you could record and have easy access to the information. So, let's go to the next step!

Customer's Emotional Profiling Process

Now, it's time to develop the emotional profile you need. It actually starts the process of separating your business from your competition. In today's marketing world, most business owners are trying to be all things to all people. They believe they need to cast a wide net in order to land the most prospects but nothing could be further from the truth.

When you try to be everything to everyone, you become nothing to no one. You fail to differentiate yourself from the pack and you simply blend into the crowd. We previously discussed the three elements required for any business or start up to be successful. They are:

- Every business must stand out from the crowd and be unique.
- The business must offer exceptional value.
- The business must be able to communicate its uniqueness and value.

If you offer the same thing as all of your competition, then you're not unique nor are you offering your prospects extraordinary value. With none of these components in place, you have nothing to communicate to your prospects that will be emotionally compelling. You simply look like your competition and you will forever compete on price.

When you target a specific customer profile, you stop trying to be all things to all people. When you stop this activity, you make your business unique. You make it stand out from the crowd. As we continue building on this process, we'll also help you create exceptional value. Once we do that, you can produce compelling marketing and advertising that clearly communicates your message to your target customers.

So far, you've only defined your physical profile that makes up your target customers. Now, we can start developing the emotional profile. It's time to help you blow the lid off this process and uncover

what your target customers really want from a business like yours. Let's look at our previous example we used to define a physical profile of your target customer. Let's begin with our childcare example. Demographically, we said the ideal childcare client would be male or female; 21 to 45 years old; single or married; one to three kids between the ages of three months to five years old, employed outside the home, and have an annual income somewhere between $20,000 and $250,000 per year. So essentially, all human beings on the planet with kids under six that work and don't have friends or relatives that can watch them during the day, need the services of a childcare facility.

That's their physical makeup. But what do they really want? What is their emotional profile? What problems, frustrations, fears or concerns are they feeling as they consider placing their child in the custody of strangers? What would you be experiencing emotionally if you were in their shoes? Please don't take this exercise lightly. This may be one of the single most important exercises you will ever perform for your business by far. It could also be directly responsible for either business success or failure. If you only spend a few minutes completing this exercise, your business may end up paying a heavy price.

As a successful entrepreneur or business owner you must develop the ability to step into the actual shoes of their target customer. This may be one of the most important skills you develop and it can have a major impact on the bottom line of your business. In fact, your entire marketing program rests on the outcome of this one exercise. So we encourage you to give this your all.

You must learn how to think like your prospects. You must learn how to tap into their mindset and feel what they feel on an emotional level. You must know and understand what their emotional switches are; how they face their problems, fears, anxieties, frustrations and concerns. You must be able to empathize with them in their decision making on who they will buy from and how and what they choose to buy. You must position yourself so they will buy from you and not your competitor. The digitalization era allows savvy business owners to leverage on automation so they can track customers behaviors and emotions. That is where the monetization on digital social platform comes in. It offers a perfect approach in studying the emotional profile as well.

In childcare, look at the physical profile process we presented for you to follow. We asked you to consider three different types of clients. We requested that you begin with your youngest possible client, then a client that fell in the mid-range age bracket, and then finally, a client in the upper-age bracket. The reason for this segmentation is simple. These different segments will typically want different things from your business.

Let's say you're a parent, twenty-one years old and you and your spouse just had your first child who is three months old. You both work all day and you have no reliable childcare options. You're young and you just entered the workforce. You both find yourselves in entry-level jobs making entry-level wages. Your combined annual income is only $40,000.

So what do these young adults want from a childcare facility? What's going through their minds as they contemplate leaving their precious newborn with complete strangers for eight hours each day? What are they feeling emotionally? What fears, frustrations or concerns race through their minds? What would you be feeling and thinking if you were in their position? Are you beginning to see why this is one of the single most important skills you can acquire as an entrepreneur or business owner?

If you can train yourself to think and feel the way your target customers think and feel, and then innovate your business so that you give them what they want to help them overcome their fears and concerns, they will instantly buy from you and keep coming back for more.

There is an entire universe of prospects that need your product or services. But within that vast universe, you have different segments that want different things. You must identify every single want and then select the one that you have a purpose and passion for serving. That one area is often referred to as a niche market. If you perform this exercise to the best of your ability, you will be able to quickly identify all the available niche markets for your target customers and then select the one that's the right fit for you and your business. But first, we need to identify the ones that exist within your available universe of prospective buyers.

Consider the situation if you were a young parent with a newborn baby and the only option you have is to leave your child with a childcare facility. What would you want from that facility? As a young parent you probably don't make much money. Based on that fact alone, most young parents want childcare that's extremely affordable; more like a glorified babysitting service. The cost of the childcare will typically be their main consideration and their major emotional switch.

But let's say you're a thirty year old parent with a child in the age range of three months to three years. You've just received a major promotion in your company and your new position comes with a hefty raise. You just went from a $45,000 a year income to $70,000. For the first time in your life, you have some discretionary income. The first thought for you would be making a better life for your child. So think for a moment, what would you want from the childcare facility where you leave your precious child nine hours every workday?

Since the child is three years old or younger, most parents of young children want specialized childcare. They want the staff at the facility to show their child extra love, care and attention. They want each staff member to treat their child as if they were their own. They would also be willing to pay more to acquire that type of child-care.

After all, if you were in this same position, wouldn't you want these things for your young child? The younger parents could not afford this type of upscale childcare facility. So affordability will typically be their main consideration. But for the thirty year old parent who now finds themselves in a much more affluent situation, finding childcare that specializes in providing close supervision along with a loving, caring, nurturing environment becomes their number one emotional switch.

But what if you were in your forties and made an executive level income? What if you were a forty year old business owner or executive making a comfortable mid-six figure salary and your child was three to five years old? Would you want something different from childcare than our previous two examples? Again, put yourself in their shoes. Their child is older and school is rapidly approaching. Most parents begin to think in terms of education. They would love to see their child receive some form of preliminary education that could give their child a head start in preschool.

If you were in this situation, wouldn't you prefer a childcare facility that offered beginner reading skills, beginner math skills, or possibly basic computer skills as options for parents? If you agree, and educating young minds stirs a purpose and passion in your soul, this would be your big opportunity to innovate your day care and offer parents this unbelievable, one-of-a-kind option. Your childcare facility could even offer a written guarantee that all children in this program will be reading at a first grade level before they entered kindergarten. Do you believe parents in this specific situation just might be interested in a childcare facility like this for their older children?

Here's the point behind this exercise. When it comes to childcare, there's a universe of prospects that need it, but within that vast universe lies a multitude of prospects with situations they specifically want and those desires are heavily tied to their feelings and emotions. They are basically divided into these three specific and highly defined segments. That's why the next step of identifying our target customer, involves carefully defining these segments which we call our niche market.

Target Market Segmentation

Let's identify the specific segments that define the emotional desires of our prospects. What is it they really want from our product or service? For childcare, there are three distinct and completely different niche markets that define this industry: affordability; a nurturing, loving environment; and educational opportunities. Identifying these upfront offers the savvy business owner a major opportunity to create a business that stands out from the competition and one that can quickly dominate their entire market. This will be the subject for this section. This same situation applies to a small and medium sized business development or a digital marketing agency.

Their job is to help entrepreneurs or business owners build their dream business. We previously identified their target customer's physical profile. They focus on business owners and entrepreneurs. These businesses may be in start up mode. Or they may be established businesses with a year or more under their belt but they aren't pleased with their growth rate. They may want to develop faster, or they may be stuck at a specific income level and frustrated by their inability to move their business off this plateau. They could also find themselves in major financial trouble and fear going out of business.

These businesses typically have 20 or fewer employees. If they're a start up, they must have a viable concept or an established business plan in place for the business coach or consultant to use as a road map. For the typical small sized business, their gross revenue seldom exceeds $3 million. So when the business development coach or consultant describes the physical profile of their available universal prospects, it's essentially every small sized business under $3 million in annual revenue. Today, that equals to more than 30 million businesses in just the U.S. alone. But emotionally, what do more than 30 million businesses want from a business development or digital marketing agency? What are the problems, frustrations, fears and concerns that are impacting them emotionally? What type of support do they need to solve their emotional switches? Let's take them in order.

The start ups and businesses that are less than a year old with less than $3 million in revenue need to generate leads and increase cash flow fast. Most of the businesses fitting this profile are in the fight of their life just to keep the doors open. These businesses are simply looking for a way to make payroll week to week and increased revenue and cash flow are the top trigger issues. The five-year-old mid-size business with revenue from $3 million to $50 million and five to fifteen employees wants the agency to help them grow their business to the next level. They want to put a process in place that allows them to operate their business with total confidence. They want peace of mind to train others to run their business even if they cannot physically be there.

The medium businesses with $50 million to $100 million usually have working systems and processes already in place. They have documented company policies and procedures and a staff that's typically well trained in executing those procedures. They have marketing that typically generates an adequate number of monthly leads and revenue. These business owners want a business development agency to help them replace themselves so that they can spend more time with friends and family instead of living at work 24/7. They too want to ensure their business doesn't implode if they aren't there. When it comes to digital marketing, these business owners will want to take all the frustrations and guess works out their life so they focus on what they do the best.

Can you see a pattern forming here? For businesses selling to both consumers and businesses, in every case, there's a massive available universe of prospects that need what these specific businesses sell. But within that vast universe lies specific emotional profiles that divide them into specific niche markets. Unfortunately, the vast majority of business owners and start ups never take the time to go through this profiling process and carefully identify their prospect's emotional switches. They do not see how innovating around those emotional switches can benefit their business. This knowledge could lead to them being the only business that offers these specific prospects exactly what they want.

Many business owners don't consider ways to address those triggers and how they can communicate to their target customers and prospects how they offer solutions. It's every business owner's job to identify and define the most important emotional switches that top their prospect's list. They must identify the things their prospects want from their business and lead them to look to their business for solutions to their problems, frustrations, fears, and concerns. Informed business owners understand the importance to list all of their target customer's emotional components and then select the one that resonates most with their purpose and passion.

The next section will help you focus on selecting your specific niche market and stress why it's so important to the future growth of your Business. Remember, all of your prospects want to feel special. They want to feel that they are working with the expert who has the products and services that can help them solve their problems, address their concerns, alleviate their fears and frustrations for good.

Let's assume that your prospects are tired of seeing cookie cutter businesses that all offer the same products or services but they don't come close to giving them what they truly want. In other words, they are desperately looking for a unique business that stands out from the crowd. They want a business that understands them and gives them what they want. They want a business that also offers them exceptional and extraordinary value. And if you believe that you can provide them with such a business, they'll reward you by paying you a higher price for what you sell as long as the value you offer justifies the price they pay.

They also want you to communicate with them in a loud, clear, and easily understandable voice. They want your message to clearly communicate to them that you are different and you do offer exceptional value. They're tired of searching and they will appreciate a clear, concise message that doesn't play games. Instead, your message and business highlights the benefits you provide specifically for them. And if your business provides these three major elements, you will see prospects show up in droves. When you establish yourself as a unique business which offers exceptional and extraordinary value and clearly communicates those benefits to your prospects, you will literally dominate your entire niche market.

Let's say you're looking for a personal trainer. You can call ten trainers who offer the same services. The promise is to help you add lean muscle mass, lose weight, feel better and add energy. In other words, they are trying to be everything to everyone. As a result, they become nothing to no one. But if you call a trainer and they tell you that they specialize in just one thing; helping people over 40 add ten pounds of lean muscle mass within 30 days through a specialized proven and tested workout program that only they provide, they have just separated themselves from all other trainers.

By developing this specialized focus, they've made their business unique and simultaneously created massive value to the individual prospects that are looking for this type of trainer. All that's left is for them to effectively communicate that message to their target prospects that will quickly react to this emotional switch. As you can see, the emotional profile is about 90% of the entrepreneur business success experience. The emotional profile identifies what your ideal clients really want when they buy your product or service. When you give them what they want in a unique way that's loaded with value, you've just made your business the logical choice. Using this model, we equip business owners all over the world to discover their target market and dominate their marketplace. This is also the process we use to help these small and medium business owners reach the multi-million dollar revenue level.

Assignment on Customers' Emotional Profile

Building a multi-million dollar business is not mission impossible. Anyone with a purpose and passion for what they do and who commits to the business fundamentals in building their business can do it. The process we're presenting to you is a step by step approach to building a successful and highly profitable business. It all starts with developing your strategic position and target customer profile.

Your job is to first identify the physical profile for your target customer and then identify their emotional profile so you thoroughly understand their emotional switches. Some prospects may only have one emotional switch while others may have ten. If you're passionate about serving the prospect with the one emotional switch, that automatically becomes your niche market. If there are multiple emotional triggers, then you must select the one that you have a true purpose and passion for serving. This will become your niche market.

We'll work more on this in our next section, but for now we'll stay focused on identifying your prospect's emotional switches. Now, go back and review your physical profile and then create a list where you ask yourself:

- When it comes to my product or service, what could the prospects in my physical profile possibly want that would compel them to buy what I sell?

- What are the possible problems, frustrations, fears or concerns that actually exist for my product or service?

Using the clients' cases in this book as a guide, transfer both your physical and emotional profiles into the related form in the end of the section. List the physical traits in the box at the top and the emotional traits in the box on the right.

Review the examples for guidance. If you struggle with this exercise and find it difficult to identify emotional switches for your target customer, try talking to them. Approach your current customers or prospects. Ask them to tell you their biggest problems, frustrations, fears or concerns about buying what you sell or will sell.

Our previous client, Right Image Photography conducted his survey and discovered that price was not critical and that clients loved his creativity. Even if you believe you know your clients' emotional switches, consider verifying them. You may discover that your numbers are off or that you had the triggers listed in the wrong priority. Most business owners list low price as the typical prospect's number one issue only to discover, after speaking with these clients, that price was one of their lowest concerns.

Next, we're going to help you select your niche market. This is where you focus on the 20% that will bring you 80% of your revenues and separates your business from your competition. From here, you just have to keep building upon these steps to establish your unique position in the marketplace.

Our main purpose of this section was to help you develop a solid foundation as you build a highly successful business. That foundation demands that you identify and understand your target customer. We highlighted two major factors that will help you to identify your target customer:

- Their physical profile makes up only 10% of the business success journey since it identifies the available universe of prospects that need what you sell.

- The emotional profile makes up the remaining 90% by identifying who wants what you sell. When you hit your prospect's emotional issues, they will instantly pay attention to your message.

So take your time and complete the physical and emotional profile assignments. Use the examples in the book as guides and then record your information on the attachment forms in the end of the section. Remember, these things are foundational building blocks to help you get what you want; a successful, profitable business.

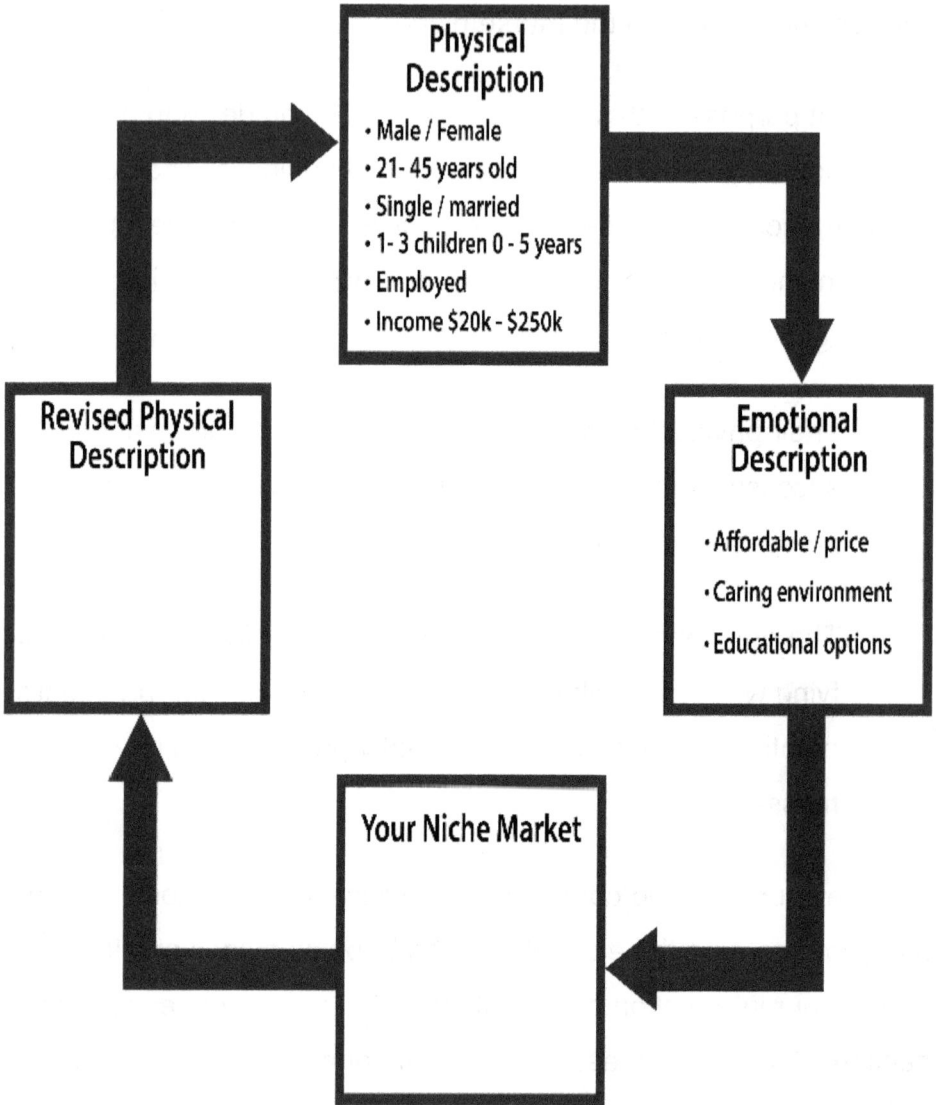

Physical Description

- Male / Female
- 21- 45 years old
- Single / married
- 1- 3 children 0 - 5 years
- Employed
- Income $20k - $250k

Emotional Description

- Affordable / price
- Caring environment
- Educational options

Your Niche Market

Revised Physical Description

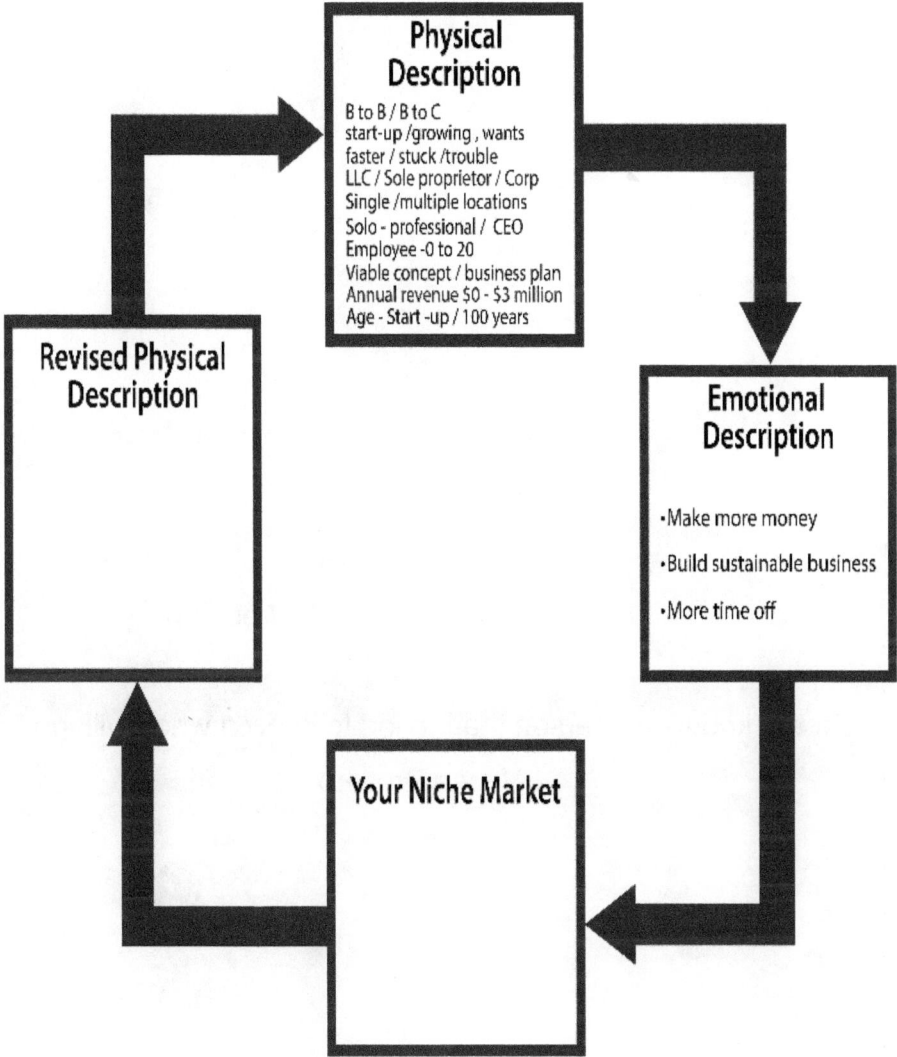

Physical Description

B to B / B to C
start-up /growing , wants
faster / stuck /trouble
LLC / Sole proprietor / Corp
Single /multiple locations
Solo - professional / CEO
Employee -0 to 20
Viable concept / business plan
Annual revenue $0 - $3 million
Age - Start -up / 100 years

Revised Physical Description

Emotional Description

- Make more money

- Build sustainable business

- More time off

Your Niche Market

SECTION FOUR

Develop Your Niche Market

"Better know one person than trying to know a whole village."

- African Proverb

SECTION FOUR
Develop Your Niche Market

This section continues our process of developing your ideal client profile. Remember that it one of the most critical important business fundamentals that directly impacts the ultimate success of your business. If you follow the instructions, this section could represent a major turning point in both the life of your business and your life as an entrepreneur or business owner. In taking this fourth step, you will be selecting the niche market that resonates most with your ideal client as well as with your individual purpose and passion.

So why is this important? Let's say you happen to see your competitor's marketing and it looks exactly like your marketing. In fact, most of their ads say the exact same thing as your plan. They have the best price, excellent quality, great customer service. They've also been in business for twenty-five years and offer a satisfaction guaranteed benefit. Here's the problem. When you look like your competition, you're doomed to forever compete on price. It is human nature to want the best deal and it doesn't matter what you buy. Everyone wants to feel that they're getting the best deal. Fortunately for you, the best deal doesn't always mean the lowest price.

Believe or not, price is one of the last things most prospects consider. But when you look exactly like your competition, prospects have no way to tell who offers the best deal. They then naturally default to the business that offers the lowest price. What prospects really want is value. Who offers the most value in relation to the price being charged? Your prospects will pay you a much higher price as long as they feel the value they receive is greater than the price being charged. The only way business owners or entrepreneurs can create extraordinary value is to position their business as being unique. That means that you must stop being all things to all prospects. You must position your business into a very specific and well-defined niche market.

Once you select your niche market, you position your business for market domination. You position your business in a league all its own and it becomes the obvious choice for all prospects looking to buy what you sell. Selecting your niche market gives you the ability to pinpoint your target prospects. When you pinpoint the prospects that use your products or service, you can then produce far more focused advertising and promotional programs. You can offer more compelling inducements to motivate these prospects to buy what you sell.

Let's consider the business of a personal trainer at a health club. This trainer continuously advertises that they help people lose weight and get back into shape. There is nothing wrong with that except it is not a compelling message. Does this message literally "reach out and grab" attention? Does the message practically force someone to request their services? It probably doesn't. In fact, it sounds exactly like what every other personal trainer says that they do.

But what happens when you come across an advertisement that gives away a free eBook titled *"How an Extremely Busy Mother of Three Lost Nineteen Pounds of Ugly Fat in Just Eight Weeks And How You Can Get the Exact Same Results or Even Better."* Do you think this just might capture the attention of all new mothers facing this common problem? Do you think they would respond in droves for the information? Of course they would!

The E-book could highlight of all the major benefits you provide that cater exclusively to new mothers. You could include a specialized diet plan tailored specifically for their body type and hectic schedule. An exercise plan these mothers can easily incorporate into their daily routine while the baby sleeps is a bonus. You can also detail how your club provides babysitting services with childcare certified staff members.

If this was your business, do you believe that these mothers would want to hire you as their personal trainer? But think about this for a moment. Wouldn't ninety-five percent of all the content in the E-book apply to most people across the board? How difficult would it be to slightly alter that E-Book, change the title to, *"The Only Step-By-Step Fitness and Weight Loss Program Designed For The*

Bride-To-Be That's Guaranteed to Get You in The Dress of Your Dreams." Do you believe this might attract prospective brides-to-be?

Since we're into content development, what if we alter this again and add another new title to the cover that reads, "*The Only Step-By-Step Fitness and Weight Loss Program Designed for Prospective Grooms Guaranteed to Have You Looking as Good as Your Bride on Your Big Day.*" Wouldn't this instantly grab the attention of any man about to take the big plunge?

But why would this work so much better than simply saying, "I help people lose weight and get back into shape?" The answer is simple. Prospects today want expertise. They want to do business with the best of the best. Just saying you help people lose weight and get back into shape sounds just like every personal trainer on the planet. There is absolutely no incentive for me or anyone else to take action. After all, I can get this service just about anywhere from anyone. But when you start specifying new moms or brides-to-be or prospective grooms, you've positioned yourself as the specialist in those markets. As a result, you position yourself as the dominant authority and win the majority of the business.

These specific areas are called niche markets. Positioning your business in a specific niche market is your key to massive business success. Don't forget that we've included attachments forms in the end of the section. It will help you to reinforce the information we'll be covering and act as an ongoing resource you can review in the future.

Identifying and Selecting Your Niche Market

We've already discussed the basic process required to help you identify your ideal client profile. We discussed the process you need to discover your demographic and psychographics profiles. Now, we want to help you identify and select an appropriate niche market; one that caters to your purpose and passion while positioning your business as unique.

Let's quickly review why an ideal client profile is so critically important for your business. We will also see how selecting a niche market changes everything about your business and how it enables you to build the business you've always wanted. You must first identify your ideal client's demographic profile.

Demographics describe the physical components of the universe of available prospects who need what you sell. These traits are important since you will use them later to find and market to your ideal clients. But, as we know, demographics alone are only responsible for approximately 10% of the business owner's success. The remaining 90% of your success is determined by your ideal client's psychographics profile.

The psychographics identify what those available prospects in your universe want or desire. We often refer to the psychographics as your prospect's emotional switches. They describe the problems, frustrations, fears and concerns that your prospects have when they buy what you sell. They define the emotions your prospects are experiencing and what solutions you offer that attracts them. In most cases, emotional switches are not dependent on an individual business. They tend to be the same for every business in your market.

Let's take a look at going to the dentist. When you visit the dentist, what immediately frustrates or concerns you? One factor could be the typical long wait before we're seen by the dentist. Then we need to complete paperwork we may have filled out 100 times before. This is aggravating.

Let's take a look at your car. What happens when something goes wrong and you need a mechanic? When you think about it, you experience immediate frustration, concern and fear thinking about the possible cost of an arm and a leg to get it repaired. You also think about being held captive by thoughts of paying much more than what you've budgeted.

Can you see how these triggers are not related to any specific business? They're common to the entire industry. Everyone shares in these same emotions whenever these specific situations show up in their lives. These are the psychographics that entrepreneurs, business owners, startups and marketers must know, understand, and conquer. This explains why the psychographics determine the success or failure of your marketing program. **Remember to stay away from manipulating your prospects and clients with the emotional switches.** That will be a straight path to failure because you may not be able to deliver the value after you have their attention.

Since your prospects buy based on emotion, they're looking for the business that will take the emotional issues out of their lives forever. The business owner who does that will have a customer for life. That's why the psychographics represent 90% of your potential success. The demographics define the prospects that have a logical need to use your product or service but the psychographics define the prospects that have an emotional reason to buy and desire what you sell.

When you know and understand their emotions, you can then create messages that target their desires; powerful messages which are emotionally compelling. These messages will resonate deeply within your prospects and attract only those who want what you sell and compel them to take a specific action. But these messages or message must be specific in order to be effective. The dentist can't just say that their practice offers fast service for the busy patient. That's called a platitude. No one believes them, usually because this message may be false. You may visit this dentist and find out that you wait just as long as you do at your previous dentist appointments.

When you know and understand the specific psychographics that resonate with your ideal client, you then create a message that thoroughly convinces them to buy what you sell. Imagine the dentist's marketing saying something like this. "I understand how busy my patients are today and waiting is the last thing you have time to do. That's why I offer a no wait guarantee for all my patients. I see every patient within five minutes of their arrival or they don't pay for their appointment." Do you believe them?

This dentist is putting his money where his mouth is. Now, the question is, can this dentist deliver on that promise? They better be able to do just that. That may require them to innovate their practice to implement this offer. Can you see how powerful it would be if their practice could execute this offer? They could then dominate their market.

Waiting is a major psychographics trait or major trigger for prospects looking for a dentist. Demographically, we all need dentists at some point in our lives, but what we really want from the dentist is to be seen at our exact appointment time. The potential impact this marketing message can have on your business is enormous and immediate. It's a message that instantly attracts your ideal clients.

They will spend the most money with you, buy from and stay with you forever, love your product or service, share your purpose and passion for what you do, send you referrals, and provide you with endless testimonials.

Now, let's shift to an auto mechanic. If you find a mechanic who has fair pricing, who provides you with excellent service and honest estimates and who has never overcharged you, do you ever want to leave that business and try someone else? Of course, you don't! That's because each of these traits are emotional switches for all prospects that need auto repair work. If your prospects find a business that takes away the pain of auto repair, they will never leave. It simply comes down to knowing and understanding the emotions of your ideal clients. But as you just witnessed with the automotive mechanic, quite often, your ideal clients want several things from your business.

You may have discovered the same thing when you completed your business psychographics work. Unfortunately, as we shared earlier, most business owners, marketers and entrepreneurs try to be all things to all people. The result is, they become nothing to no one. They now look exactly like their competition. When everyone looks identical, prospects have no way to tell which business offers the most value. That's when they automatically default to the business offering the lowest price.

The purpose of this fourth step is to help you stop trying to be all things to all your prospects. If you try to be everything to everyone, there is no way for you to prove that your business is unique and that it offers extraordinary value. Finding and selecting your niche market changes all of that for your business forever.

Selecting Your Niche Market

Previously, you completed your target market physical profile (demographic) and emotional profile (psychographics) form. On the psychographics side, you recorded everything your universal prospects would conceivably need and want from your product or service. You may have listed a few things they want. The number doesn't matter. What does matter is what type of business you want and who you want to serve. The well known 80/20 life principle applies here as well.

When you operate a business and you spend your valuable time speaking and working with prospects all day, shouldn't you enjoy it? You owe it to yourself to be happy and to capitalize on that unmistakable passion you have for what you do. This, in turn provides your clients with a unique experience and extraordinary value.

We'll help you take the psychographics information listed on your form, and extract from the emotional switches listing. We'll also help you to select the niche market that best matches and resonates with your true purpose and passion. Let's look at our five previous clients case study examples and discuss the potential niche markets that exist for each business. If you recall, three of our business case studies sold to consumers; a day care center, a jeweler and a consumer attorney. The other two businesses sold to other businesses; a business attorney and a business development/ digital marketing agency. We will also discuss the obedience dog trainer as an added bonus from a peer to peer team member.

So let's begin with our day care business and go through the entire process and reinforce the importance of developing your ideal client profile. Earlier, we identified the ideal day care client as either male or female, twenty-one to forty-five years old, single or married, and have one or two children between the ages of three months up to five years old. They are also employed outside their home, with an annual income somewhere between $20,000 and $250,000 per year. In other words, any human being with children under six years old and works outside their home needs day care services.

But then we asked ourselves, what do those parents want? What is their psychographics profile? What are their emotional switches? What are their problems, fears, frustrations or concerns? What reality do they face which is forcing them to place their young child into the hands of strangers? What are they experiencing emotionally? Actually ask yourself, what would you be experiencing if it was you?

Here's a major point that we believe needs emphasis. We regularly tell entrepreneurs, business owners and start ups that one of the most important skills they can learn and perfect is the ability to temporarily suspend their mindset and step into the mindset of their ideal client. It is crucial that you master this skill.

One of the biggest factors for a business failure is what we refer to as the curse of knowledge. As a business owner, don't you know every facet of your business? That's often a curse because you know so much that you make assumptions. You assume your prospects know what you know. Making those assumptions can destroy you as a business owner or entrepreneurs. You must learn how to think like your prospects think.

An important question to ask is what's really going through their minds? What are they feeling and experiencing emotionally? What emotional switches are at play? What problems, fears, anxieties, frustrations and concerns are they facing as they decide whether or not they will buy what you sell.

When you created your demographic profile, we asked you to consider three different types of clients. We asked you to define with your youngest possible clients; clients in the mid range age bracket and finally a client in the upper age bracket. If you sell to other businesses, we asked you to consider the age and size of the business in terms of both revenue and employees. The reason we asked you to segregate them is that these different client segments desire completely different things from your business.

Daycare Case Study

Let's take a look at the demographic profile of a day care center and the available universe of human beings who need their services. You can see the different age levels represented and that they each want different things. Young parents are just getting started in the workforce and most of the time, find themselves in entry level jobs making entry level wages. Their total annual income may be in the range of $40,000 more or less. Young parents, as a rule, usually don't have a lot of money so they want a day care that's affordable.

Emotionally, price will be their main consideration. That's their top emotional switch. But if you're a 30-year-old parent with a child three months to three years of age, you recently received a promotion to a management position. You have an average, yearly income of around $70,000. You would most likely want a day care that will not only treat your child with care but also has operating hours that fit your busy schedule. You would also want day care that provides a loving, and nurturing environment and you'd be willing to pay more for that type of day care.

However, if you are a forty year old business owner or executive, making a comfortable six figure annual income your expectations are different. You have a child who is three to five years old and rapidly approaching preschool age. You want your child to receive preliminary education that would give them an educational head start. You want your child to receive beginner reading and math skills or even basic computer skills.

When it comes to day care, the point is that there is a single demographic universe that needs day care, but within that universe is a multitude of psychographics and desires that divide that universe into specific segments. It's imperative that you define these segments and see how they apply to your specific business. But once you do, you must make a choice. You must select the one segment that you want to focus on and identify as your niche market. It's time for your business to stop trying to be all things to all people. As a day care owner, it's time to stop trying to say you can serve all three segments, everything they want, because you don't. In fact, you can't or you will fail with your marketing programs. Once your business growth is sustainable, serving the different segments is an option.

How can you hire staff members with specialized skills and certifications in preschool education who can provide a nurturing environment for children and still claim to be the low price provider in your day care market? There is no way you can do this. But that's what many day cares do everyday all over the country. They advertise that they have the highest quality, the lowest prices and well-trained staff. The problem is, they can't offer definitive proof. Prospects only learn the truth by wasting time and money when they use their services. Even worse, their competition says the exact same thing. day care prospects have difficulty differentiating any of it and lean to the one offering the lowest prices.

Prospects call around and quickly discover that most day care prices are the same. They have the exact same staff-to-child ratio. They serve the same bland foods and the television acts as the primary babysitter. It's not what these parents want. If you are the owner of this day care, you must realize there are three different and entirely distinct groups considering your services. Each of these groups want something completely different from the others.

By selecting just one of these three groups and then creating a day care that specializes in serving only that one specific group, you now have a day care that's unique and it stands out because it is different from all the others. You deliberately chose to leave the other two groups on the sideline. For those prospects that fall into your selected group, you will attract every one of them in your location. You have exactly what they want. None of the other day cares offer what you offer and you can continue innovating.

Here are a couple questions. Which of the three segments do you select as your niche market? Which one becomes the single focus of your business? Although this is an individual choice based on the preference of the business owner and the marketplace, here's our personal recommendation. Never make this decision based solely on the amount of revenue you make on a specific niche market. Please do not misunderstand. We know revenue is an important factor. Just don't let it become the sole factor in your final decision. Focus on offering a valuable solution and money will follow.

Now, look over the available niche markets on your list and select the one that most resonates with your individual purpose and passion. Which one excites you the most? Which one of these groups are you willing to dedicate your life to meeting their needs? Which group gets you so excited that you wake up every morning and can't wait to get started? Which one causes you to wake up thinking about what you do and go to bed each night thinking those same thoughts?

Purpose and Passion are the keys to selecting your niche market. Without it, you will hate what you do and resent those you serve. If you let money alone dictate your choice, you will feel no passion for your labors. Life is too valuable to sacrifice your joy and happiness for a few extra dollars. As a rule, when you follow your purpose and passion, money often comes along for the ride. When you're passionate about what you do, you're constantly thinking of new ways to improve and innovate while building your business. This in turn attracts more and more clients and adds additional revenue and profit to your bottom line. If you own a day care, it would be good to confirm your real purpose and passion. Do you have a passion to help young parents faced with the bleak prospect of placing their young child in daycare? Would you find unbridled joy in providing low cost day care to young parents even if you can only give them the bare essentials to keep the price low? Would you be able to offer them enough services to give them complete peace of mind?

Do you have some special training or a degree that your competition doesn't have? What is your past experience? Have you done something that gives your business a substantial advantage over your competitors? Are there any price advantages you have such as special deals, an exclusive wholesale supplier or some form of acquisition that your competition can't match?

Let's look again at your purpose and passion for providing a low cost day care option to young parents. You may actually have a competitive advantage when it comes to a low cost option, but what is it? Let's say that you recently inherited a two-story brick building and it is mortgage free. As an added bonus, this building requires little to no modifications in order to house a day care center. Since you have no mortgage payment factored into your expenses, you have an economic advantage over other area day care centers. Another advantage is that this building sits squarely in the middle of a major office complex. The location alone will bring you as many clients as you can handle without incurring any advertising expense.

These competitive advantages matched up with your purpose and passion for providing low cost day care services to young parents in your community, offers you the best of both worlds. But what if you have a passion to provide a nurturing environment as your niche market? Ask yourself what competitive advantages you have in this area.

Perhaps you have a degree in health and nutrition and you have the unique ability to create nutritionally designed meals in a day care atmosphere. You can also offer a day care with a low staff-to-child ratio. It ensures the children get more individual attention. You also have a certification to provide onsite training for the staff. On a side note; this is a comparative advantage we built for our client Wisdom Senior Care.

Because of your specialized training, you have a day care that re-quires staff to attend monthly onsite safety and CPR training class-es. In this case, you consider your purpose and passion first. Your background and past experience acts as an added benefit and gives you a competitive advantage that other day cares can't match. What parent looking for a nurturing environment wouldn't want a day care operated by a certified trainer?

But what if your purpose and passion is to provide a day care that specializes in educational opportunities? In this case, you can find your competitive advantage exists because you have a degree in primary education and you know others in this field who are young mothers. These mothers would welcome the opportunity to teach part-time. This benefit enables them to earn additional income and spend more time with their own child who attends your day care. Just imagine the impact of working onsite with their child in the same building. Their child could not only attend the same day care but they would be surrounded by other children.

Matching your purpose and passion with your competitive advantage gives you a huge competitive edge in this market. But remember, when you select your niche market, you should always first consider your purpose and passion. You can take a serious look at your other competitive advantages only after you initially consider your passion and purpose.

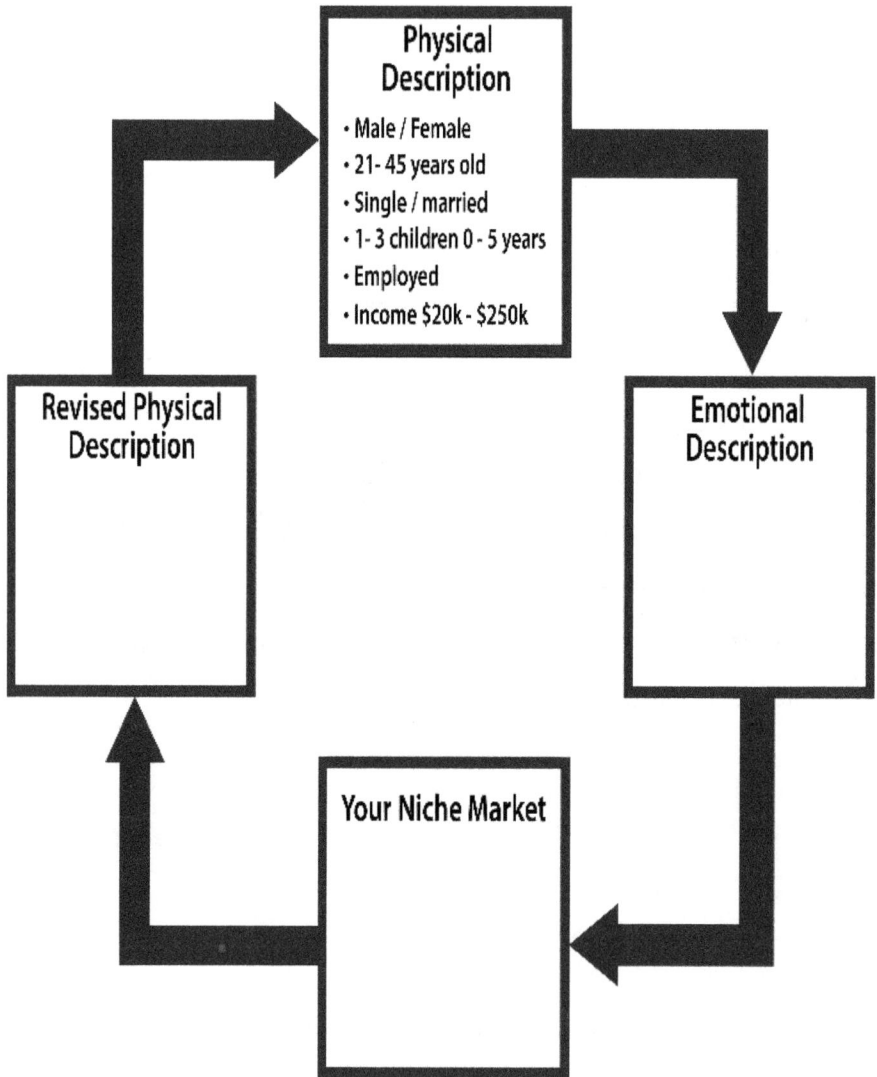

```
                    ┌─────────────────────┐
                    │     Physical        │
                    │    Description      │
                    ├─────────────────────┤
                    │ • Male / Female     │
                    │ • 21- 45 years old  │
                    │ • Single / married  │
                    │ • 1- 3 children 0 - 5 years │
                    │ • Employed          │
                    │ • Income $20k - $250k │
                    └─────────────────────┘
```

Physical Description

- Male / Female
- 21- 45 years old
- Single / married
- 1- 3 children 0 - 5 years
- Employed
- Income $20k - $250k

Revised Physical Description

Emotional Description

Your Niche Market

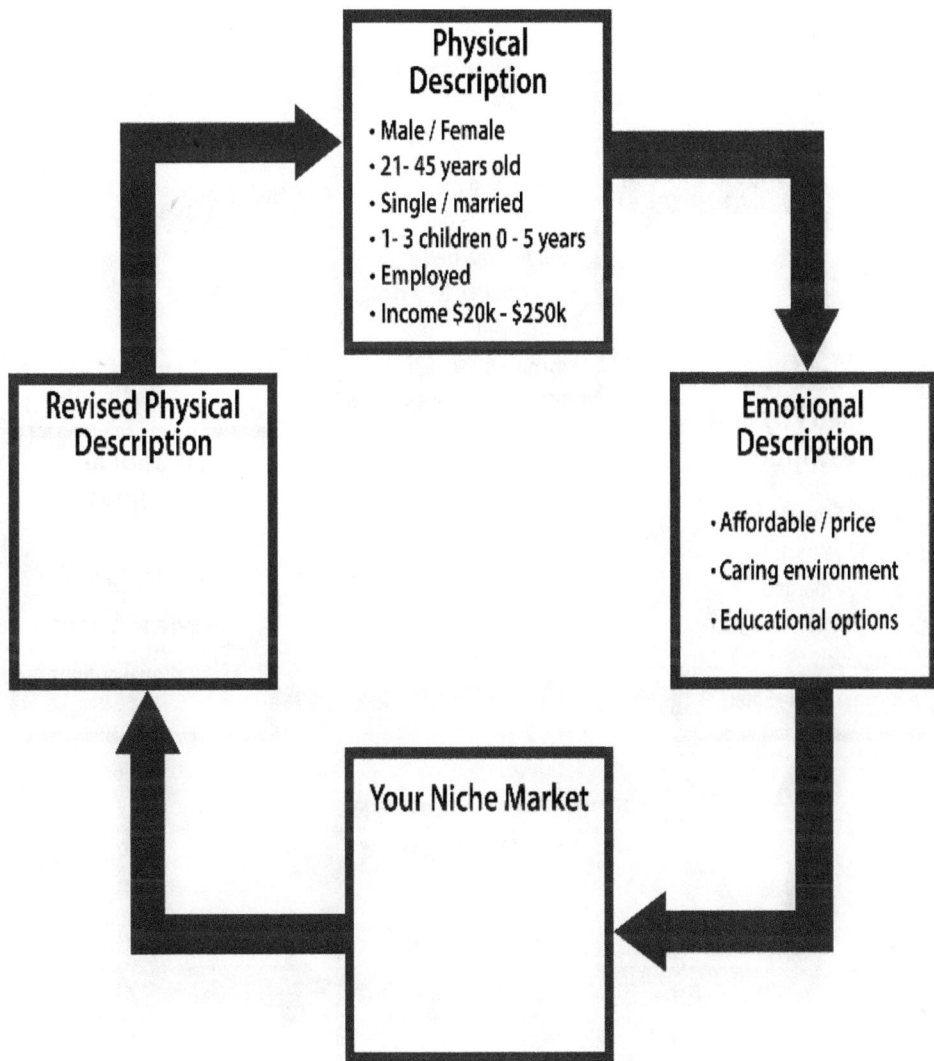

```
                    ┌─────────────────────┐
                    │     Physical        │
                    │   Description       │
                    │ • Male / Female     │
          ┌────────►│ • 21- 45 years old  │─────────┐
          │         │ • Single / married  │         │
          │         │ • 1- 3 children 0 - 5 years   │
          │         │ • Employed          │         ▼
          │         │ • Income $20k - $250k│
┌─────────┴────────┐└─────────────────────┘┌─────────────────────┐
│ Revised Physical │                        │     Emotional       │
│   Description    │                        │   Description       │
│                  │                        │                     │
│                  │                        │ • Affordable / price │
│                  │                        │ • Caring environment │
│                  │                        │ • Educational options│
└──────────────────┘                        └─────────────────────┘
          ▲         ┌─────────────────────┐         │
          │         │  Your Niche Market  │         │
          └─────────┤                     │◄────────┘
                    └─────────────────────┘
```

Physical Description

- Male / Female
- 21- 45 years old
- Single / married
- 1- 3 children 0 - 5 years
- Employed
- Income $20k - $250k

Revised Physical Description

Emotional Description

- Affordable / price
- Caring environment
- Educational options

Your Niche Market

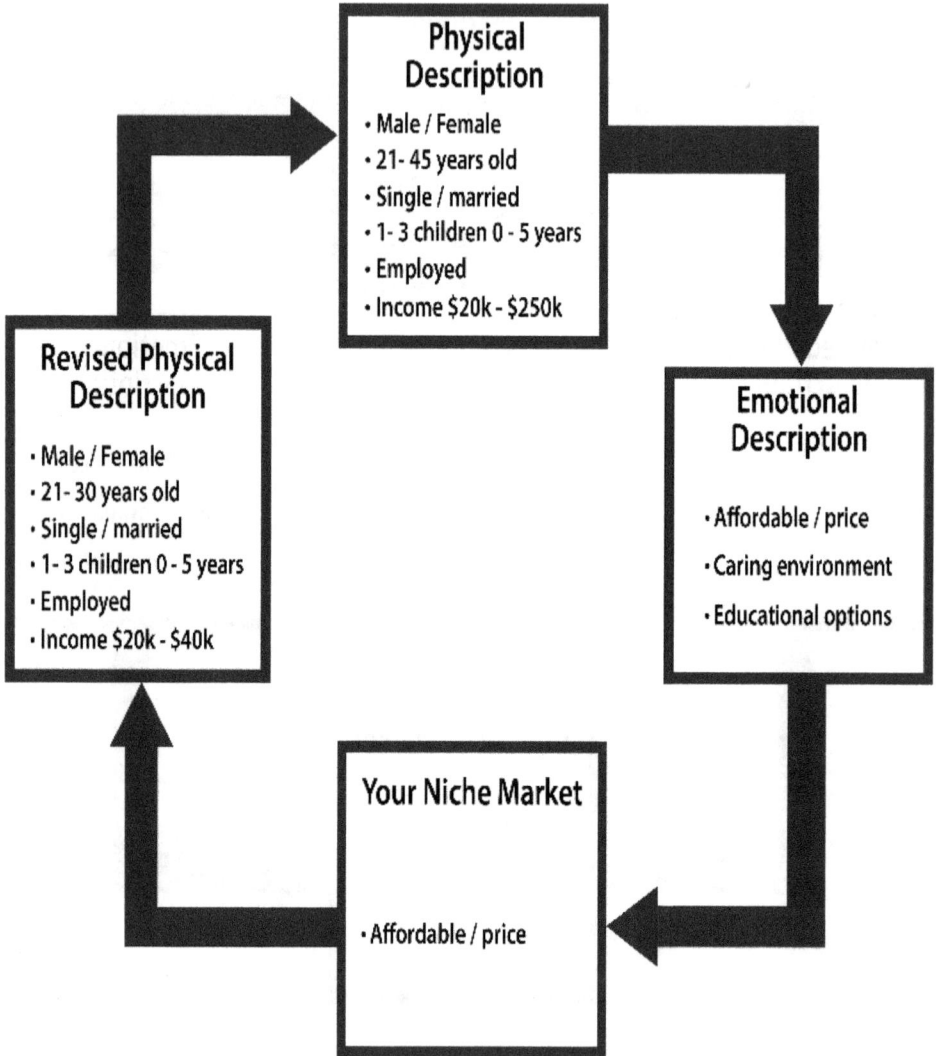

Physical Description

- Male / Female
- 21- 45 years old
- Single / married
- 1- 3 children 0 - 5 years
- Employed
- Income $20k - $250k

Emotional Description

- Affordable / price
- Caring environment
- Educational options

Your Niche Market

- Affordable / price

Revised Physical Description

- Male / Female
- 21- 30 years old
- Single / married
- 1- 3 children 0 - 5 years
- Employed
- Income $20k - $40k

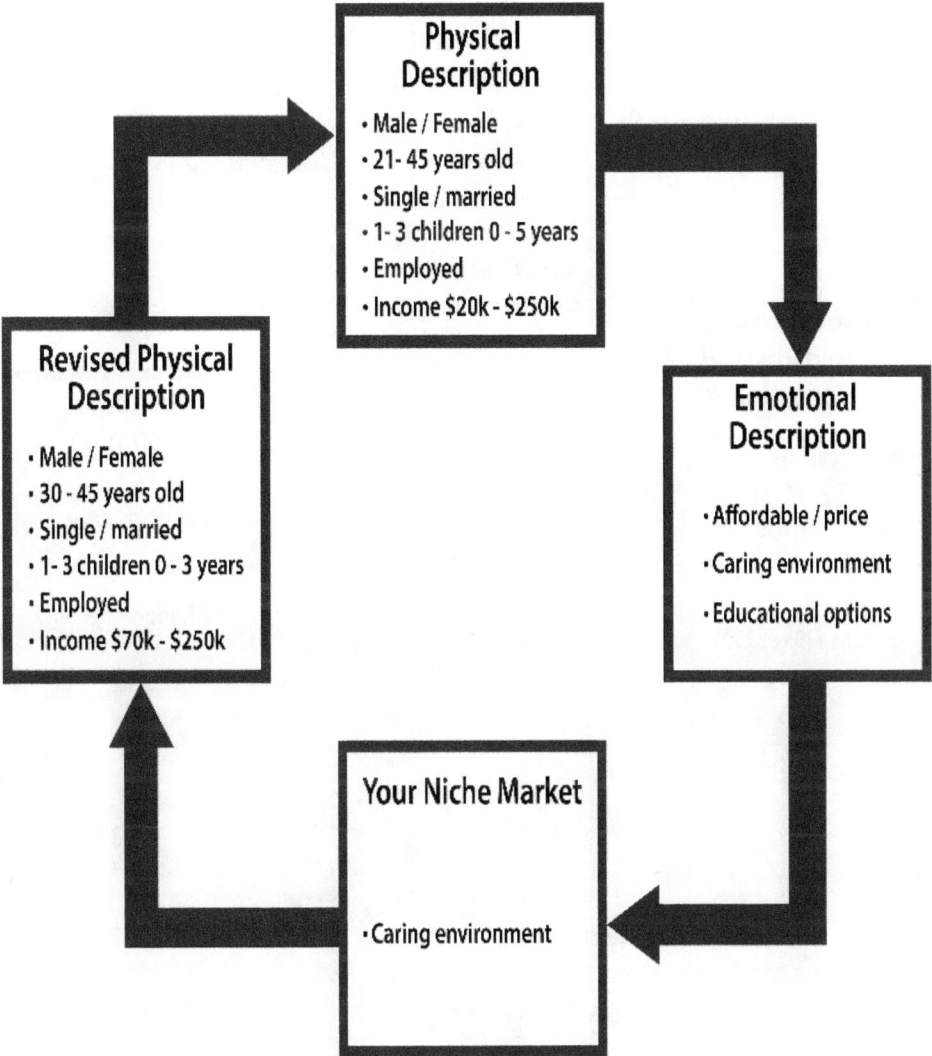

Physical Description

- Male / Female
- 21- 45 years old
- Single / married
- 1- 3 children 0 - 5 years
- Employed
- Income $20k - $250k

Emotional Description

- Affordable / price
- Caring environment
- Educational options

Your Niche Market

- Caring environment

Revised Physical Description

- Male / Female
- 30 - 45 years old
- Single / married
- 1- 3 children 0 - 3 years
- Employed
- Income $70k - $250k

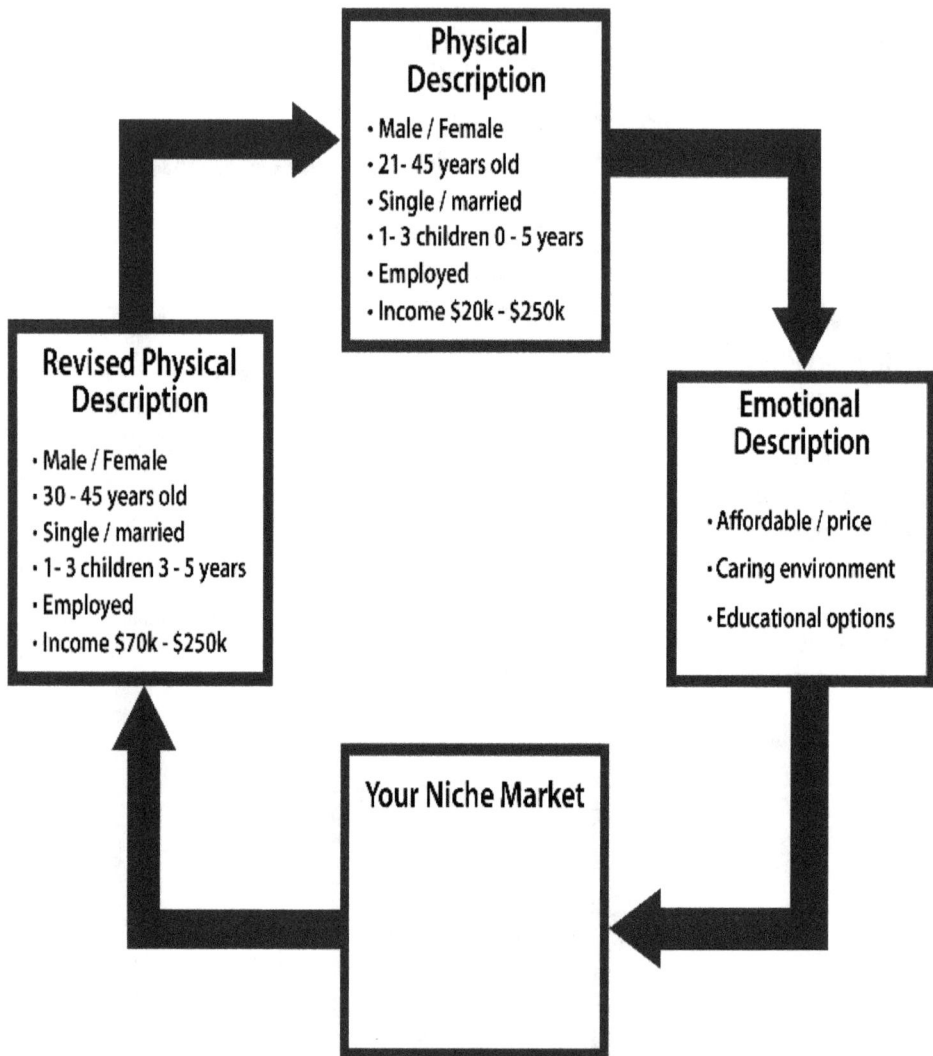

Physical Description

- Male / Female
- 21- 45 years old
- Single / married
- 1- 3 children 0 - 5 years
- Employed
- Income $20k - $250k

Emotional Description

- Affordable / price
- Caring environment
- Educational options

Your Niche Market

Revised Physical Description

- Male / Female
- 30 - 45 years old
- Single / married
- 1- 3 children 3 - 5 years
- Employed
- Income $70k - $250k

Jeweler Case

Let's look at a case study of a jewelry store located on Main Street in Clayton, NC. They primarily deal with watches, rings and bracelets. One of our team members used their services to repair his diamond sprinkled watch. After researching the owner's story and observing their ads, we chose to elaborate this case study for the purpose of the book to add value to any jewelry business owner. Assuming that working with diamonds is their specialty, demographically, their prospects universe is made up of both men and women, twenty to eighty years old, single or married, generally employed with an annual income ranging anywhere from $20,000 to millions.

This describes the available universe of humans who want, at some point in their lives, to purchase a diamond from a jeweler. Now let's ask some questions. What do they want? What is their psychographics profile? What are their emotional switches? What are the problems, frustrations, fears and concerns they experience as they consider buying a diamond?

We'll use the same process as we used before. Let's start with our youngest demographic. What do they want from a jeweler? Isn't it logical that price and affordability are primary triggers for them? In fact, they would not only be concerned about the price but they also want an affordable payment plan since most prospects in this younger demographic may not be able to afford to pay in full for even inexpensive items.

Let's change the scenario and consider a forty year old married woman or man preparing to celebrate their fifteenth wedding anniversary. The husband may want to purchase his wife a diamond tennis bracelet or the wife may want to purchase her husband a diamond watch. They are older and have more discretionary income. They may also be in a position to easily afford a higher priced item. They want to know they're receiving the highest quality and best value for the price they pay. They're not looking for the

Lowest priced diamond. They're looking for the diamond with the most value. As long as the value is worth the price, they are willing to make the purchase. Now, let's consider a sixty-five year old married man preparing to surprise his spouse with a diamond ring for their 40th wedding anniversary or his spouse who wants to surprise him with a diamond watch. What do they want? Over the years, they may have given each other several different diamonds in various configurations. They both want something different and completely unique. They may also consider a custom-made or a one-of-a-kind item.

Price would not be one their top emotional switches. In fact, for something unique, they expect to pay a premium price. This is what they want. You can see three completely different types of prospective clients all wanting different things from a jeweler. Again, we see a single demographic universe that needs the services of a jeweler, but within that universe you can identify a multitude of psychographics and desires that divide that universe into specific segments.

A savvy jeweler does not try to serve all three markets. Instead, they select their niche market from this list of three diverse segments; affordability, quality and value or unique custom-made one-of-a-kind items. Again, purpose and passion should be the driving forces followed by any competitive advantage they have in the one area they select.

Ideally, it would be great for a jeweler with passion for providing the lowest price to have a relative who is a diamond wholesaler who could sell to them at cost. Another option is they sell their products from home. That would completely eliminate costly overhead. The jeweler with a passion for providing high quality and valuable diamonds could also have specialized skills in analyzing unique quality traits in diamonds that other jewelers can't match. This skill gives them the ability to recognize and bid on these diamonds and pick them up at a favorable price.

The jeweler with a passion for uniqueness may have years of experience designing and producing one-of-a-kind items for a specific industry. They would have clients in high profile industries like entertainment. But they can offer that talent to a general consumer market. In every case just mentioned, the purpose and passion, background and past experience of each jeweler gives them a competitive advantage that other jewelers can't match.

Attorney to Consumer Case

Remember the attorney who offers legal services? Demographically, their ideal clients are men and women, eighteen to eighty years old, single, married, divorced or widowed, employed or unemployed with a household income between $20,000 and $1.5 million annually. So essentially, everyone of legal age, at some point in their lives will need an attorney. But what do our individual groups, both young and mature want from an attorney? What psychographics apply to this universe of prospects?

The eighteen year olds are still exploring their youth as they transition from teen to adulthood. They may want the services of an attorney primarily for traffic violations and DUI arrests. But those that fall between the age of twenty-five and forty, want an attorney to review their mortgage and real estate contracts when they buy their first and sometimes second homes. At this age range, some may be already establishing their estates. The forty to fifty year olds want an attorney to create wills and set up trust funds for their children. The people over fifty want an attorney to help set them up proper financial planning for long-term security when they retire. In our present culture, there is an increasing rate of divorce and these different groups may want an attorney to handle a divorce.

Again, we see a single demographic universe of consumers that needs the services of an attorney. But within that universe there is a multitude of psychographics and desires that divide the universe into specific segments. The attorney who selects a specific niche market based on their purpose and passion, background and experience instantly positions themselves as unique. In other words, they will specialize in just that one niche market. They will be able to offer extraordinary value to their clients along with any competitive advantages they have in their practice.

Attorney Services to Businesses Case

The same situation applies to the attorney who offers their legal services to business owners. Let's review the demographics for them. At some point, what type of businesses need the services of an attorney? They could be businesses just starting up or they may have been established for one hundred years. The businesses just starting may have zero in revenue, whereas the ones with years in business may have $100 million in revenue. The startup may be owned and operated by a solo professional with no employees in a single location, while the older business may have a CEO, three thousand employees and locations in twenty separate locations.

The startup may be a sole proprietorship or an LLC, the owner of a majority corporation. They may sell a product or service, or in some cases, both. So demographically, any business on earth at some point may need the services of an attorney. But what will these businesses want from an attorney? What are the psychographics that apply to this large and diverse group? What niche markets do they need to review to make their selection?

If your business model is to sell business-to-business, begin with the most relevant factors that have the most influence when those businesses buy what you sell. Those factors include the age and size of the business both in terms of revenues and employees. A startup with no revenue and zero to five employees want an attorney to help them set up their corporate structure and create a business plan. A couple of years old business with less than $1,000,000 revenue and few employees want to start adding employees. They want an attorney to create their employee handbook, legal employment contracts and protect their rights and assets.

A five to ten year old business with $1 to $10 million in revenue and five to fifteen employees may want an attorney to set up profit sharing for their employees, provide guidance as they create an HR department and set up a retirement plan. A ten year old business with more than $10 million in revenue and more than fifteen employees may want an attorney to assist with their expansion plans, intellectual property advice, or even in the implementation of an exit strategy. So when a business-to-business situation is present, we still see a single demographic universe of business owners that need the services of an attorney. But within that universe lies a multitude of psychographics and emotional switches that divide that universe into specific segments.

By selecting their niche market, this law firm positions itself as a specialist. If they have additional competitive advantages to offer, they'll be viewed as an expert. In fact, business owners demand specialization even more than consumers do. The product or service a business owner purchases often has a direct impact on their clients. That impact reflects directly back on them and their business. For example, a business owner hires an attorney to develop a binding contract which requires another business to purchase a product on a scheduled basis. Upon completion, the contract contains misspelled words and incorrect terms and conditions. That incompetence reflects back on the business owner and not on the attorney who wrote it.

This is the major reason business owners don't like dealing with businesses that try to be everything to everyone. They not only want the specialist. They want the expert.

Business Development and Digital Marketing Agency Case:

This same situation applies to any business services provider. The agency's job is to help entrepreneurs, business owners to build the business of their dreams. Their demographic profile includes businesses that sell to both consumers and other businesses. The businesses that come to them for help can be in startup mode developing, but they want to accelerate their growth rate. They're often stuck at a specific plateau and have no idea how to take their business to the next level. They could also be in the midst of financial difficulty and find themselves in serious economic trouble. They are looking to leverage on the digital tools to reach more prospects.

The typical agency sweet spot would be a business with fewer than twenty employees and have a viable business concept if they're just starting. Their gross revenue is zero to $3 million. So demographically, a business development and digital marketing agency's universe can be essentially any small and medium business with under $3 million in annual revenue.

There are around 30 million businesses just in the U.S. alone. But emotionally, they have to know what these 30 million businesses want. What are the emotional switches that create their problems, frustrations and concerns as they operate their businesses? What solutions can the agency offer to help solve their problems or eliminate their fears and concerns? Some of these businesses need some quick revenue. At this stage of business, each day is a struggle to survive so they want the agency to help them *make more money*. At the same time, digital marketing is a frustrating process for them. They know they have to move to the digital world, but how do they do it?

That's their psychographics, one emotional switch. The mid-sized business in the five year old range with $3 to $50 million in revenue and five to fifteen employees wants the agency to help them build a sustainable and scalable *business*. Now that they're established, they want help developing a *sustainable process* that sets their business up for *long term success*. But larger and more established businesses often have their systems and processes in place. These business owners want the agency to guide them to replace themselves so they have more valuable time with loved ones instead of living on the job 24/7. They want to ensure their business doesn't implode if they aren't on site. They are thinking more about legacy.

Are you starting to see a pattern? For both consumers and businesses, in each case, there's a single demographic universe that needs what each of these specific businesses sell. But within that universe lies a multitude of psychographics and desires that divide their universe into specific segments. These segments are what we refer to as a niche market.

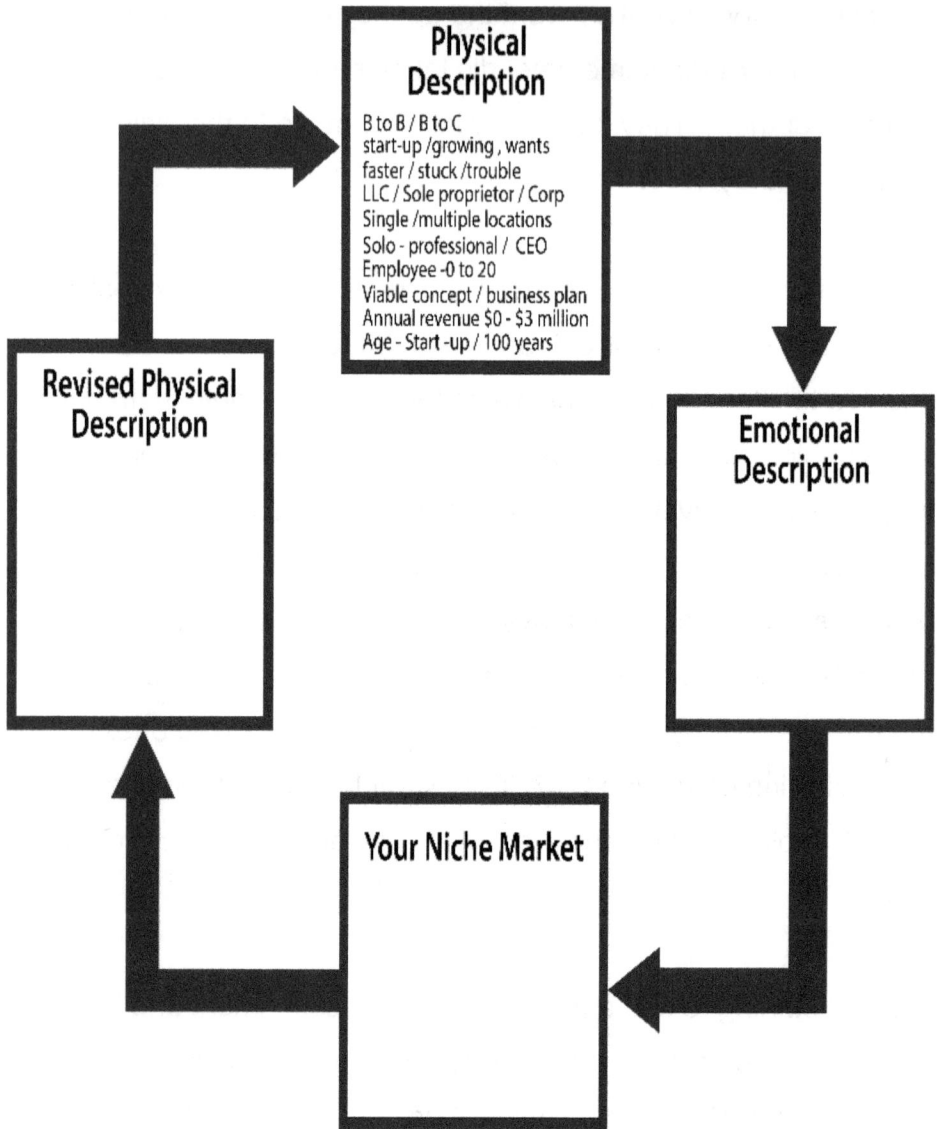

Physical Description

B to B / B to C
start-up /growing , wants
faster / stuck /trouble
LLC / Sole proprietor / Corp
Single /multiple locations
Solo - professional / CEO
Employee -0 to 20
Viable concept / business plan
Annual revenue $0 - $3 million
Age - Start -up / 100 years

Revised Physical Description

Emotional Description

Your Niche Market

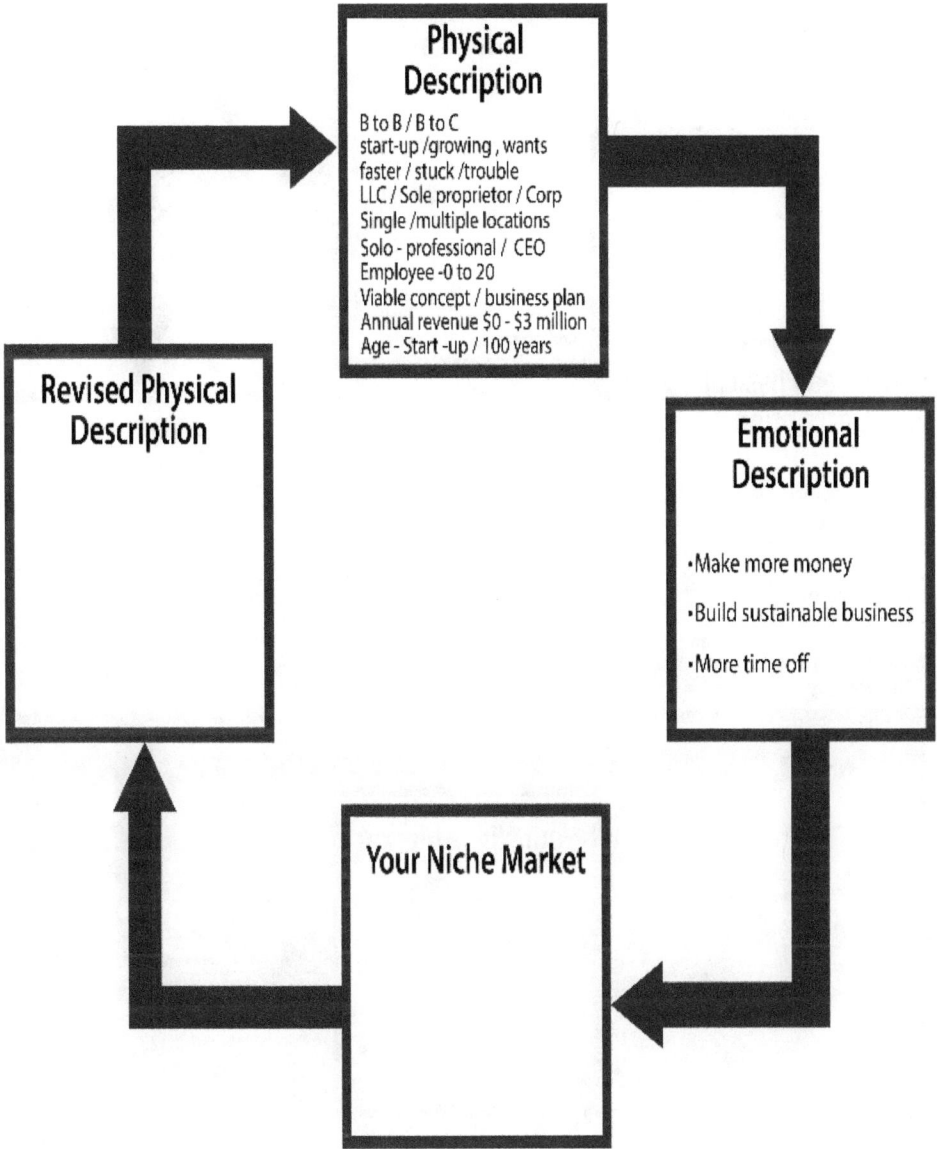

Physical Description

B to B / B to C
start-up /growing , wants
faster / stuck /trouble
LLC / Sole proprietor / Corp
Single /multiple locations
Solo - professional / CEO
Employee -0 to 20
Viable concept / business plan
Annual revenue $0 - $3 million
Age - Start -up / 100 years

Emotional Description

- Make more money

- Build sustainable business

- More time off

Your Niche Market

Revised Physical Description

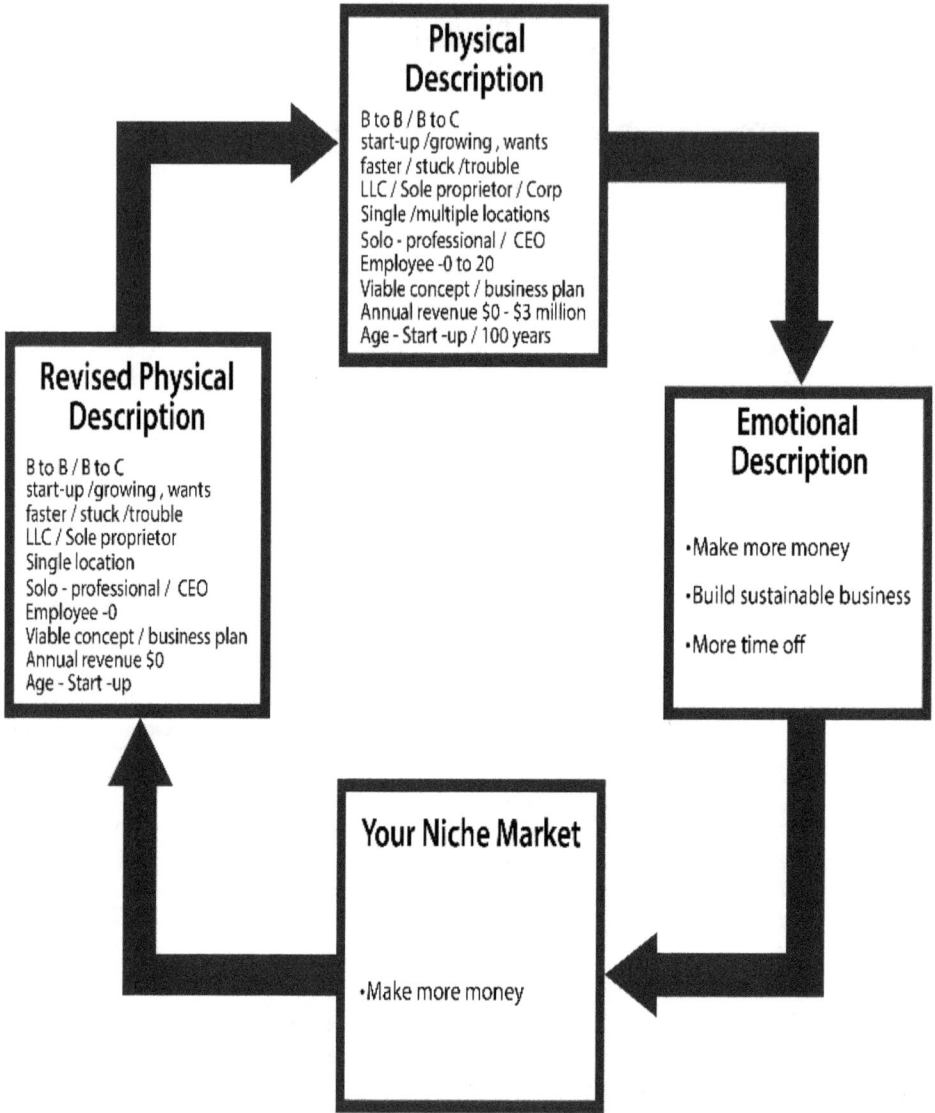

Physical Description

B to B / B to C
start-up /growing , wants
faster / stuck /trouble
LLC / Sole proprietor / Corp
Single /multiple locations
Solo - professional / CEO
Employee -0 to 20
Viable concept / business plan
Annual revenue $0 - $3 million
Age - Start -up / 100 years

Emotional Description

• Make more money

• Build sustainable business

• More time off

Your Niche Market

• Make more money

Revised Physical Description

B to B / B to C
start-up /growing , wants
faster / stuck /trouble
LLC / Sole proprietor
Single location
Solo - professional / CEO
Employee -0
Viable concept / business plan
Annual revenue $0
Age - Start -up

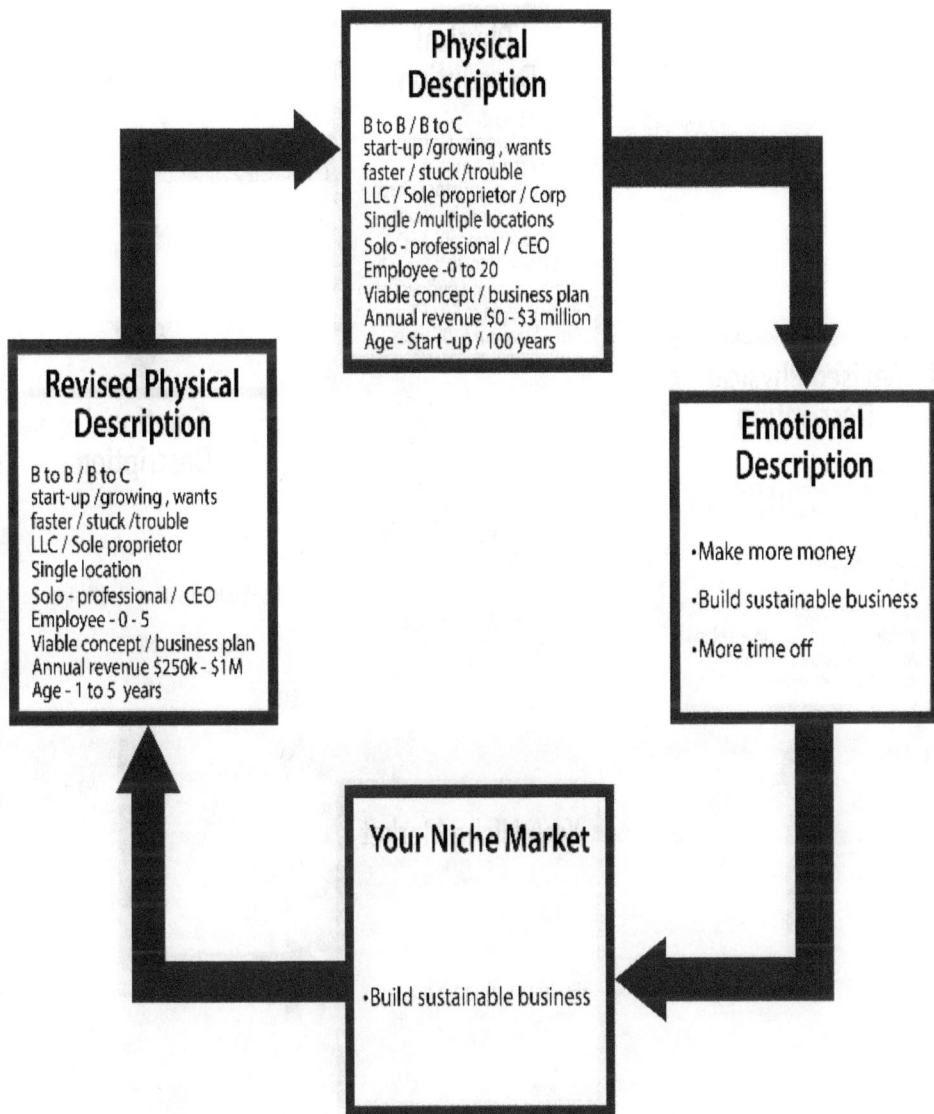

Physical Description

B to B / B to C
start-up /growing , wants
faster / stuck /trouble
LLC / Sole proprietor / Corp
Single /multiple locations
Solo - professional / CEO
Employee -0 to 20
Viable concept / business plan
Annual revenue $0 - $3 million
Age - Start -up / 100 years

Emotional Description

• Make more money

• Build sustainable business

• More time off

Your Niche Market

• Build sustainable business

Revised Physical Description

B to B / B to C
start-up /growing , wants
faster / stuck /trouble
LLC / Sole proprietor
Single location
Solo - professional / CEO
Employee - 0 - 5
Viable concept / business plan
Annual revenue $250k - $1M
Age - 1 to 5 years

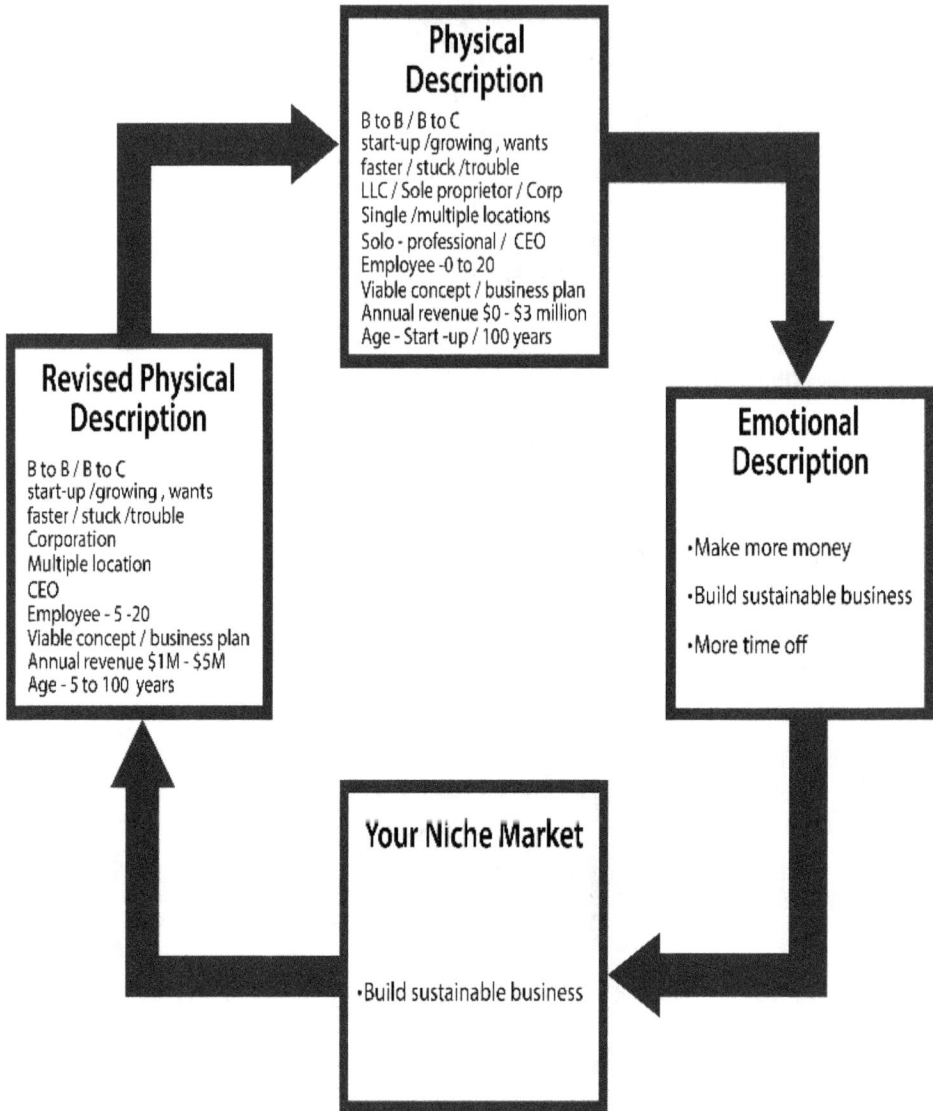

Physical Description

B to B / B to C
start-up /growing , wants
faster / stuck /trouble
LLC / Sole proprietor / Corp
Single /multiple locations
Solo - professional / CEO
Employee -0 to 20
Viable concept / business plan
Annual revenue $0 - $3 million
Age - Start -up / 100 years

Revised Physical Description

B to B / B to C
start-up /growing , wants
faster / stuck /trouble
Corporation
Multiple location
CEO
Employee - 5 -20
Viable concept / business plan
Annual revenue $1M - $5M
Age - 5 to 100 years

Emotional Description

• Make more money

• Build sustainable business

• More time off

Your Niche Market

• Build sustainable business

Dog Trainer Case Study

We promised to apply the same process to a dog trainer. We developed this case study after meeting PawzLife Inc, an organization working on identifying dog waste with their DNA to reduce dog waste on the ground in our communities. While this may sound unimportant, it is a critical facet of the community. Pet waste can carry harmful bacteria, parasites, or viruses. That's the reason its important to educate pet owners to clean up after their pet. When pet waste is left on the ground, rain and snow melts and can carry the toxins to storm drains which leads to our lakes, rivers, and streams, often untreated. It can elevate bacteria levels and contaminate our water bodies, causing our beaches to close.

Decaying pet waste can also consume oxygen and release ammonia. Low oxygen levels and high ammonia can damage fish and other aquatic life. Similarly, nutrients in pet waste may increase algae and weed growth in our water, which consumes oxygen as they decompose which also further harms aquatic life.

Pawzlife's passion for finding a solution to dog waste, led us to following the dog trainer case. An encounter with this owner then fueled our interest in the dog training industry. The dog trainer was able to sell his business and focus on training other trainers. Upon meeting him at a business networking event, we discovered that he had a deep love and a true passion for dogs. He has a unique gift for working with animals. Many of his clients highly recommend him as a dog whisperer. He can get a dog to do almost anything and he uses love instead of intimidation to accomplish this.

When he first started, he walked dogs for $10 an hour. He said his true passion was obedience training but he didn't know how to start that type of business. There was too much competition in that market and he didn't know how to position himself to attract more clients and build a viable and sustainable business. He didn't know his ideal client profile and he was paying a steep price because of it.

He found himself trying to sell his services to people who expected him to walk their dog at no charge. Because he was acquiring any client that would hire him, he was having trouble collecting payments. In fact, several of them felt they were doing him a huge favor for just hiring him. They didn't see the value in what he was offering. He found himself feeling devalued and several clients just paid him whatever they felt like paying.

It was so bad that people were paying him far less than what they initially agreed to pay. Again, since these were not his ideal clients, the value of the service he provided wasn't realized. That was obviously very frustrating to him. This was not the business or the life that he envisioned. He felt there had to be a better way.

That's when he finally reached out to us for help. His frustration wasn't unique. We hear the same sad story almost on a daily basis from business owners. When the current condition of their business was assessed, this all stemmed from lack of developing their ideal client profile and especially the psychographics. With no ideal client profile, he only attracted individuals who needed his services. Once he took the time to create his ideal client profile, he was then able to identify who truly wanted his services. So he followed the exact process you're following.

Let's take look at his demographic, psychographics form. At the time he completed this, he was walking dogs. So who on the planet needs the services of a dog walker? What would their demographic profile look like? This group could be male or female, eighteen to eighty years old, single or married, typically employed, which is why they needed a dog walker. They could also be a retired elderly person who's not physically capable of walking their own dog. Obviously, they owned one or more dogs and have an annual income of $20,000 plus. In other words, they are everyday dog friendly human beings on the planet of legal age who own a dog, who work or are retired, and they also need a dog walker.

But emotionally, what do these prospects want? Depending on their specific situation, they may want several different things from a dog walker. They may want someone to walk their dog if they had to work late. They want a well-behaved pet that has had obedience training. They want someone they trust to board their pet if they're going out of town for an extended period of time. They might even want a service that operates like a doggy day care who offers transportation services with morning pick up and evening drop off.

These are all potential niche markets for him. He had to make a choice from all of these possibilities and select just the one that resonated the most with his purpose and passion. Naturally, he chose *obedience training*. That one decision changed his life forever. He purchased his dream home and because of his ideal clients' demands, he was able to substantially expand his business and also offer boarding services. These new services alone generated enough revenue in his first month to cover the growth of his expansion.

He worked with clients who not only respected what he was doing but they were thrilled with it. They pay him premium prices because he has a business dedicated to giving them *what they want, not just what they need*. They sent and continue to send continuous stream of referrals. In fact, he stopped marketing his services. He couldn't keep up with the demand from the referrals he received. Of course, his clients have provided him with tons of unsolicited testimonials. His goal was to sell the business to travel and focus on training other dog's trainers with his expertise all over the world.

The process helped him take a dog walking business and turn it into the business of his dreams; a business that feeds both his passion and his bank account. If a dog walker can do this, do you think you might be able to do the same? This is how we serve entrepreneurs and and business owners to build successful businesses. We emphasize this not to impress you but to express to you that building a million dollar business is attainable.

Yes, it requires a mind shift, some discipline, persistence, dedication and effort. Once you decide to do anything in life that's worth doing, it takes work. Anyone with the purpose and passion for what they do and are serious and committed to building their business can do this. We are training you as we work together in reading this book. We tailored the work for entrepreneurs, business owners and start ups who want to make some serious business moves.

Niche Market Crucial to Your Business Success

As an entrepreneur and business owner, your job is to identify and define the most important prospects desires that top your business list. In other words, the top needs and wants that attract prospects to look to your business as the solution to their major problem, frustration or concern. This is what we asked you to do several sections earlier. Then in our previous sections, we also asked you to review your target market emotional switches, prioritize them and make this all important decision regarding the niche market that serves your purpose and passion. Be sure to also take into account any competitive advantages you have for that niche market.

An informed business owner should also list all of their ideal client's psychographics components and then select just one that resonates with them personally. In other words, select the area you feel the most passionately about in alignment with your purpose. It is absolutely crucial that you do this. If you want to create a highly successful business, it all comes down to this. All prospects today want to feel special. They want to feel as though they're dealing with the expert that can help them solve their problems, concerns and frustrations. They want a business that stands out from everyone else who offers a similar product or service.

In other words, they want a business that's unique. They want a business that feels, understands them, caters to them and often offers them extraordinary value. They're also willing to pay a higher price to get this special treatment as long as the value they perceive they will receive exceeds the price they will pay. Finally, they want a business that clearly communicates to them the uniqueness and value they will receive. For the business that does all of these, your prospects will connect with your services or products and show up in droves. The business that's unique offers extraordinary value and clearly communicates these benefits and has the unprecedented opportunity to totally and completely dominate their entire market.

If I'm a parent with a child currently attending a local day care, and every day when I pick up my child, I notice they're sitting in front of the television. As a parent, this concerns me. I then wonder if this is all they do with my child all day. Do they allow the television to act as the babysitter? If my child is old enough to talk, I may ask them what they did all day in day care. If the child tells me that they watch television all day, it confirms my worst fears. No parent wants that situation for their child. At the very least, I want the staff to take time out throughout the day and at least read to my child or to have them engaged in playing games.

Knowing that the television is the focal point at this day care, you actively check out other day care centers and look for one that provides a more stimulating environment for your child. But when you contact other day care centers, all you hear are platitudes and generalities. The day care center says things like, "We read to the children frequently throughout the day. We serve the most nutritious meals," or, "We have a very caring staff." If you press them for specifics, they can't provide any. That's because they don't specialize in any of these areas. Remember, most day care centers compete on price, so they hire staff members who aren't much more experienced than the children they watch.

The staff members haven't received any specialized training and In fact, the majority of the staff will be children straight out of high school who can't find any other type of work. They're going to basically be present during the day, and that's it. That's not what you or other parents want. That's not a day care center that's unique. That's not a day care that offers extraordinary value or knows how to communicate its true benefits in a compelling way. But for the day care that follows the process we've just outlined and that you have just completed for your business, this day care now knows there are three major desires prospects look for in a day care; price, loving environment and educational opportunities.

If you chose education as your niche market, you have just become unique. You just separated your day care from all others who are competing on price. You made the decision that you won't compete on price. In fact, your day care will be twice the price when compared to others. When they contact your day care, they hear specifics, not platitudes. They hear that your day care limits television time to one single hour each day with the remaining time spent teaching your child things like basic math skills, basic reading skills and beginner computer skills.

They hear you backing up the claim by telling them that their day care actually offers *a guarantee to parents that their child will be reading out of first grade level prior to entering kindergarten*, or they receive a full refund of all fees they paid over the past year. That is how confident you are on your business delivering satisfying results. Do you think this is the day care qualified prospects want? Will price be much of a consideration? These prospects want the day care that specializes in education. When they know that's all you do and you communicate your benefits to them in specific terms rather than generalities, they then know they're working with the expert in what they want. Now, you have that prospect's undivided attention. Your message and uniqueness and value fully resonates with these clients.

The price shopper is no longer in this group. You aim your sight on this specific niche market; a niche market that demands an educational environment for their child. With your value added services and your competitive advantages, you will immediately attract the entire universe of prospects who are interested in this niche market in your area.

Now, do you understand why we've stressed the importance of psychographics over the past several sections? We've stressed that these psychographics are 90% of the business success journey. psychographics identify what your ideal clients really want when they shop for what you sell. When you not only give them what they want but also give it to them in a unique way that's filled with value, you've just made your business the obvious choice. The decision to use your business and not your competitors is now a no-brainer decision.

Assignment

Your previous assignment was to identify each of your ideal client's psychographics which are also known as their emotional switches or desires. If you did, you revealed the potential niche markets that exist for your business. Your business may have only one emotional switch of the target market or it may have several. Most often, there are multiple emotional switches present. In that case, then it's your job to select the one that you have a true purpose and passion for serving and making that your niche market.

We want you to review your previous demographic profile and then review the list you created for your psychographics profile. You have to feel comfortable that you have identified every available niche market for your business. Use our clients' case studies examples included in this book and then transfer both your target market demographic and psychographics information into your updated forms in the end of the section.

If you're struggling with identifying the emotional switches for your ideal client, then try asking them directly. Interview them and ask your current clients what they want from a business like yours. Or you can ask prospective clients if you're a startup and currently don't have any actual clients. Ask them to tell you their biggest challenges, frustrations or concerns they experience when they buy what you sell. Even if you believe you know what those desires are, consider verifying them with your ideal clients. You may discover that you've missed something or that you may have listed them in the wrong order.

Most entrepreneurs and business owners list low price as the number one emotional switch only to discover after speaking with their clients that price wasn't even a factor in their decision-making. Once you feel comfortable that you properly listed all the emotional switches, look deep within yourself and select the one emotional switch or trigger that you feel a strong passion for providing to your clients. That emotional switch combined with your purpose and passion determines your niche market.

The moment you select and prioritize it, you separate your business from every other business that sells what you sell. You become unique and you stand out from the crowd. You no longer belong to the "Me Too Business" club in the eyes of your prospects. It will be your primary focus and the others will come in as secondary or not at all.

Once you do this, everything changes in your business. You market your business differently. You create entirely different messaging; messaging that laser targets the one specific emotional switch for your ideal client versus the messaging that makes you look the same as everyone else. The way you talk to prospects and clients lso changes. All of these messages begin to attract ideal clients en masse.

We'll complete the development process for the ideal client profile by revising your demographic information to reflect your new ideal client and your selected niche market. This will be the final step in identifying your ideal client. It will massively benefit your business when you complete it.

Section Recap

Let's quickly recap what we've discussed to help you develop the solid foundation required to build a highly successful business. That foundation demands that you know and understand the identity of your ideal client. We highlighted the two major factors that identify your ideal client; the demographic profile and the psychographics profile. Knowing your ideal client's demographic profile while very important, only identifies who needs what you sell. It identifies the physical characteristics of your ideal client.

The psychographics identify who wants what you sell. They identify your ideal client's emotional characteristics which are also known as their emotional switches. When you know and understand their psychographics, you also know and understand how to compel them to buy from you by appealing to their emotions. By expressing their desires, your prospects will pay attention to your message and want to buy what you sell. They will buy because your message solves a major problem, and addresses a concern or frustration that has invaded their lives. Having an accurate psychographics profile is the key to eventually create and develop a highly successful business; one that's unique, provides extraordinary value and can effectively communicate its uniqueness and value to its prospects.

The key to creating this type of business is for you to review the emotional switches in your psychographics profile and select just the one that most resonates with your purpose and passion. That selection becomes your niche market. Once you make the selection, you position your business as unique. You stop being all things to all people and you have now positioned yourself and your business as the expert within your niche market. You will eventually convey this uniqueness in your marketing program; a marketing program that will generate real results by providing the powerful and compelling information needed to reach your prospects desires.

The proven steps covered in this book define and guide your marketing programs and messaging to your ideal clients. As we continue to build on this foundation and the provided information, remember we are developing a process for your specific business. You will be able to duplicate this multiple times and far into the future. Take your time and transfer all your demographic and psychographics onto the revised forms found at the end of this section. Select your niche market and then record your choice in the lower box on the right of the appropriate form.

Next, we'll complete this form by refining your demographic profile to fit your specific niche market. We'll be continuously referring back to this information in future sections, so don't misplace your work forms. Every step builds on the previous step, so take your time as you complete each assignment.

Go the Extra Mile, Specialize In Your Niche Market

This section will complete the process of developing your target customer profile. Remember that this is an important business fundamental that directly impacts the ultimate success of your business. This section will guide you through the revision of your original physical profile and reflect the niche market you previously selected. Completion of this first critical business fundamental may turn out to be a major turning point in both the life of your business and your life as an entrepreneur or business owner.

Let's revisit and discuss why this is so important to your business. Did you know the difference between steak and garbage is all in the presentation? Here's an illustration. During an old episode of a popular television program, a daughter brought her new fiancé home to meet her parents. The problem was that she did not inform her parents that she was bringing him home. She boldly walked in and told her parents this was the man she was going to marry. Her fiancé also happened to be twenty years her senior. Needless to say, her parents were not happy with the announcement. The fiancé sensed the tension in the situation.

Finally, when he and father were alone in the kitchen, he

Confronted him and asked why he didn't like him. The father asked the young man if he liked steak. "Of course!" was his reply. The father then described in vivid mouthwatering detail the preparation and serving of a delicious T-bone steak. You could see the young man salivate as he continued his description.

"Just envision this juicy steak being served on a trash can lid. Now, How does the steak look and taste?" The father asked.

"Not too good," the young man replied. "Son, that's how you were brought into this house; on a garbage can lid," the father said.

It all had to do with the presentation. That steak being presented on the garbage can lid ruined the experienced. He then told the fiancé it had more to do with the daughter's presentation of the situation and had nothing to do with him personally. The parents were upset with the presentation, not the person.

Now, apply this same concept to a real life situation. Think about the typical insurance agent. Does anyone ever really want to sit down and discuss insurance? When our poor friend, the insurance salesman makes a pitch to someone who's not in the market for insurance, it's like garbage; unwanted, unwelcome, smelly garbage. But when the agent can provide their customers with insurance information that can improve their lives or reduce their costs, it's like steak. So how can we create more steak and less garbage? *One word: specialize.* Instead of being a neglected and shunned insurance agent, we must work to become the expert in our chosen niche market.

Seriously position yourself in a specific niche market where you possess extraordinary expertise and then niche it again if you can. Understanding precisely who you can best serve is just as important, who you actually like and have a passion for serving. Study exactly what your customers want. Innovate your business so you can give them what they want, make their lives easier, and continue to find more and more ways to serve them incredibly well.

Specialize in Your Niche Market

But why are we making all the fuss about becoming a specialist in your niche market? Your prospects are looking for experts! In fact, customers not only diligently search for them, they demand them. The smart insurance agent who follows this advice has customers calling them instead of being forced to hunt down customers. The question is, which way would you prefer?

The topic of insurance can be complex. It's not easy to be seen as an insurance expert on every type of insurance. It's much easier to become an expert on insurance for one particular kind of customer. You can learn that customer's language, understand their problems and become good at resolving the issues they most likely face. Once you know them, you can offer them additional relevant products and services. If you're a business consultant and an expert at what you do, you can give your customers what they want by granting them access to your knowledge and processes and by creating killer content in the form of hard copy programs, CDs, and DVDs. And don't forget your digital content of E-books and E-Learning.

Once you truly understand the customer you want to serve, you can create tons of valuable free content for that niche market. Start with a blog. Create an email newsletter and front load it with a terrific auto - responder follow-up sequence. Record a regular podcast. Get a camera and create some quick, useful FAQ answers to release on YouTube. Whatever you create, make it valuable. Don't try to slip in a flimsy sales pitch. That's like serving garbage unless you happen to hit the right person at the perfect time. If you do, you risk losing your remaining prospects. Always let people know how to find you when they want to know more.

If you create valuable content, the less garbage you'll present to your prospect. Remember, it's all about the presentation. When you do make an offer, it will be a valued opportunity instead of an unwelcome sales pitch made by an annoying salesperson. Make it your mission to create plenty of steak and as little garbage as possible, because the less you look like the salesman, the more you'll sell.

Again, it's all in the presentation. Selecting a specific niche market positions you as the expert and your information presentation will have tremendous value. This is the reason we spent time helping you define your niche market and why we must now redefine your physical profile. Let's find the customers that want what you sell and you can sell them what they desire. If you master this process well, you can give them what they don' t know they want yet.

Apple has mastered this. They create futuristically. They are technology leaders and masters at discovering unknown desires in the marketplace and creating products and services that address those unknown, future desires. When you're able to do this, your prospects become lifetime customers.

Understand the Importance of Emotional Profile

Your business must be unique in order to be successful. It must offer exceptional and extraordinary value and be able to effectively communicate its uniqueness and the value to its prospects. Completing your target customer profile automatically positions your business as unique. Instead of attempting to attract anyone and everyone, you are specifically targeting a select niche market with its own unique set of emotional switches. Those emotional switches are your keys to success and wealth. By selecting your niche market, you are choosing to serve a smaller yet highly-targeted market of prospects. Each of these prospects want the product or service you provide.

By selecting this smaller base of prospects, you can innovate your business and offer them exceptional and extraordinary value and provide the solutions to their biggest problems, frustrations, fears or concerns. Since you are focused on just this one select group, you can market to them in language that appeals to them emotionally.

One of the most foremost authorities on innovation, Simon Sinek, stated that people don't buy what you do, they buy why you do it. When you selected your niche market, we asked you to make that selection based on your purpose and passion; a passion that deeply resonates within you. If you do that, your prospects who also share your passion for what you do will instantly resonate with both and be attracted to you and your business. They will view what you do as a cause and not simply a product or service.

There are reasons customers choose one restaurant over another. Two restaurants may serve the same menu but customers make their choice based on factors other than price. How often have you shopped with a retailer even though that exact same product was available at a closer location? Ask yourself what motivated you to take these actions? It always comes down to an emotional reason. That restaurant or that retailer resonates with you emotionally. It may be their customer service, their variety in selection, the way they prepare your meal by adding little touches that make you feel special. Or it could even be the way the staff knows you and calls you by name. There is something they do that sets them apart from all others.

People instantly respond to a cause that appeals to their personal values because it resonates with them on an emotional level. That's what takes place when you select your niche market. Now that you have completed that critical step, you must revisit your original physical profile where you will review that vast universe of prospects you previously identified as needing what you sell.

You can then redefine those characteristics so they fit those who want what you sell. Once you complete this step, you will position your business for market domination. You will position your business in a league all its own and your business will then become the obvious choice for all prospects who are looking to buy what you sell.

Previously, we went over the basic process that's required to help you identify your target customer profile. We reviewed the process you used to discover your physical and emotional profiles. We then asked you to identify and select an appropriate niche market; one that caters to your purpose and passion while positioning your business as unique. Now, we want to help you revise your original physical profile to reflect your new niche market.

Never forget that the physical profile defines the prospects that have a logical need to use your product or service. The emotional profile defines the prospects that have an emotional reason to buy and desire what you sell. Understanding their emotions allows you to create a marketing message that targets these emotional switches. It's an important and compelling message. It resonates deeply within your prospects, attracts only those prospects who want what you sell and compels them to take a specific action.

Attracting your target customers changes everything in your business. They spend the most money with you. They buy from you over a longer period of time. They love your product or service. They also share your passion for what you do and send you referrals. They even provide you with testimonials and stay with you forever. It simply comes down to **knowing and understanding** the emotions your target customers are experiencing. But as you discovered when you developed your emotional profile, your target customers often want several different things from your business.

Problems occur when the majority of entrepreneurs, small and medium sized business owners try to be all things to all people. The end result is that they become nothing to no one. They look exactly like their competition. When everyone looks identical, prospects have no way to determine which business offers them the most value. That's when prospects automatically default to the business that offers them the lowest price.

When you complete the development of your target customer profile, you position your business in a specific niche market. You will never again have to prove that your business is unique and that it offers extraordinary value. That's the big advantage you gain when you select your niche market.

Now, let's complete this process and look into the niche market you selected based on your purpose and passion. You can then revise your original physical profile to identify the prospects who specifically want your product or service. Within this niche market, chances are excellent that your physical profile has narrowed dramatically. This will be a huge help as you begin your marketing program. We also need to review our previous business examples and revise their physical profiles based on various niche markets selected for their business. But before we do, this I want to stress there is no right or wrong decision for selecting your niche market. The only selection criteria you use should be based on the passion you feel as the individual business owner.

Let's highlight again why choosing your niche market based on your purpose and passion is such an important consideration. Once you know the various areas within your business where prospects want different things from you, you can then narrow your focus into that specific area and have a certainty that you understand what they really desire . Once you do this, you can scan your business to ensure that you're giving them exactly what they want. But that raises another huge challenge. You can't just give your prospects what they want. What's the reason for this? What they want is often what they expect to get from you. Here's an example that showcases this perfectly.

One of our previous clients owned a window cleaning company. His marketing informed his prospects that he would make sure their windows were absolutely spot-free when the job was completed. But that's what everyone expects from a window cleaning company, right? The problem is that when he delivers on that promise and delivers spotless windows, the client will never notice that level of quality because they automatically expect a window cleaning company to get their windows spotless. When you take clothes to the dry cleaner, don't you expect to get them back dry-cleaned? When you go to a restaurant, don't you expect good service? In fact, the only time you actually notice the service is when it's not good.

In other words, you just automatically expect it. It is the same thing for the window cleaning company. The only time you notice the quality of their work is if your windows are not spotless. This example highlights one simple fact about business: *you must exceed your prospects and customers' expectations to get them to notice you.* It is only when you exceed expectations that you begin to provide exceptional and extraordinary value. That's when you have the opportunity to dominate your market. That's why every business owner must look for ways to innovate their business after the four steps we covered.

Revise the Physical Profile

So let's complete your target customer profile. Revise your original physical profile by looking at our clients' business examples so you can use them as models for your own business. We have also included some filled forms in the end of the section for later reference. Let's start with the child care facility with our clients Right Time Kids in Raleigh North Carolina or the British School of Lome in Togo (West Africa) an international school we worked with 8 years ago. Let's go through the entire process to reinforce the steps required when developing your target customer profile. Physically, we originally defined the target childcare customer as either male or female, twenty-one to forty-five years old, single or married, one to three children between the ages of three months to five years old, employed outside the home and with an annual income between $20,000 and $250,000 per year.

In other words, any human being with children under six who works outside the home and doesn't have any other sources of childcare and needs the services of a child care facility. But then we ask ourselves these questions. What do all these parents want? What is their emotional profile? What are their emotional switches? What are the problems, the fears, the frustrations or concerns they have as they begin to face the reality of placing their young child into the custody of strangers? What are they experiencing emotionally? This is where you want to focus and look at these various situations from the perspective of your target customer.

Business owners often assume their prospects know what they know. Making those assumptions can destroy your business. You must learn to think like your prospects think. Just ask yourself. What's really going through their minds? What are they feeling and experiencing emotionally? What emotional triggers are in play? What problems, fears, anxieties, frustrations and concerns are they facing as they try to decide whether or not they will buy what you sell?

When looking at a child care, you see that prospects want different things. Some want an affordable price. Some want a loving environment and others are looking for educational opportunities. It's imperative that as a child care provider, you define these segments. But once you do, you must choose the one you're most passionate about with a purpose. You must select the one segment that you want to specialize in and the one you want to represent your niche market. Whichever niche market you select, you must look back at the original physical profile and revise any characteristics that may have changed. As an example, let's say as a child care provider, you selected affordable price as your niche market. Does that niche market have any impact on your original physical profile?

The original profile listed both men and women. Chances are good that both genders want low cost child care services, so that physical trait stays the same. But now, instead of an age range between twenty-one and forty-five years old, the majority of parents wanting a low price child care facility favor younger parents who just aren't making as much income at this point in their life. So physically, we need to revise this age range to twenty-one to thirty years of age. Single or married, one to three children between the age of three months up to five years of age and employed outside the home are still valid characteristics.

But the $20,000-$250,000 annual income now drops dramatically. It would be more in the range of $20,000-$40,000. When you revise your physical profile based on your specific niche market, you dramatically narrow the available prospects that fit that niche market. This also makes them much easier to find when you market to them. But what if this child care provider selected a caring environment as their niche market?

What would their revised physical profile look like? The genders, marital status, number of children and employment status all remain the same as the original profile. But notice what changes now. Providing child care with specialized services such as a loving environment become more expensive than child care that offers basics babysitting services. A child care facility specializing in providing a loving environment will be required to offer a much lower staff-to-child ratio, a nutritionist preparing daily meals, and mandatory staff training and safety. They may also have frequent staff rotations to ensure mentally alert staff which prevents adult burnout when dealing with children.

Instead of appealing to twenty-one to forty-five year old group, a caring environment caters to prospects who can afford for these more expensive child care services. These parents are earning much more discretionary income and their age will reflect that increase. A revised physical profile would be thirty to forty-five years of age. The child's age then comes into question. Most parents want child care that offers a loving environment when their children are three months old to about three years old. These are critical years for children emotionally. So that physical trait changes from our original and the income level must now be revised since child care of this type will be approximately twice as expensive as the affordable child care. The average annual income increases to $70,000 to $250,000.

But take a look at another situation. The exact same physical profile also applies to parents who want educational options but with one critical exception. The parents who prefer a child care facility that offers educational options have children between three and five years old, probably because they know their child will be starting school shortly and they want them to be well-prepared. Everything else on their physical profile remains the same as the parents who want the loving environment.

But let's explain the huge opportunity this now provides to the child care provider. A childcare facility is a physical location that parents drive to each day to drop off their children. No parents want to see themselves driving ten plus miles every day for childcare. They want a facility that's close to their home or office so it's convenient for them to drop off and pick up their children in the evening.

So when this child care facility markets their services in mass advertising venues like the newspaper, radio and television, it just doesn't make much sense. No matter how exceptional the childcare is, the majority of people seeing mass advertising won't be interested in a facility that isn't close by. So, this child care provider would be wasting their marketing dollars using these venues.

The only sensible marketing strategy for a local child care facility is to use direct mail. But how easy is it to use direct mail? Now that we revised our physical profile, you would need to purchase a mailing list from a list of broker in order to use a direct mail strategy. Naturally, the more names you buy, the more expensive the list becomes. Not to mention the price of the mailings themselves. But thanks to our revised physical profile, the child care provider only needs the names of prospects fitting their revised physical profile that live within a five mile radius of their child care facility since most parents won't be willing to drive any further than that each day.

Can you see the challenges of trying to mail to every prospective parent within a five mile radius that fits the description of your ideal client? Attempting to mail to all parents who are employed outside their home with children from three to five years old with the income between $20,000 to $250,000 per year would be daunting and expensive.

But look what happens to the marketing campaign cost when those physical traits become much more redefined. With a child care facility offering a caring environment, they only need the list with the names of parents between the ages of thirty to forty-five with children under the age of three and they make $70,000 or more. That eliminates a considerable number of parents of the total potential prospects within that five mile radius.

It's the same for the childcare offering educational options. They only need the names of parents between ages of thirty to forty-five with children ages three to five years old and they make $70,000 or more. That eliminates a huge number of parents of their potential prospects as well. Do you now see why we spent time creating your target customer profile? Once we do this properly, it enhances everything regarding your business.

When you select your niche market, you often disqualify vast numbers of prospects that you may otherwise attract. Unfortunately for most of them, you won't be offering what they want. This means you waste your time and effort trying to sell your product or service to prospects that may need what you sell but don't desire what you sell.

Selecting your specific niche market allows you to innovate your business to fit the wants of that specific market so you not only offer qualified prospects what they want but you give them more than what they want. They see you providing them with exceptional and extraordinary value and they will come to you en masse.

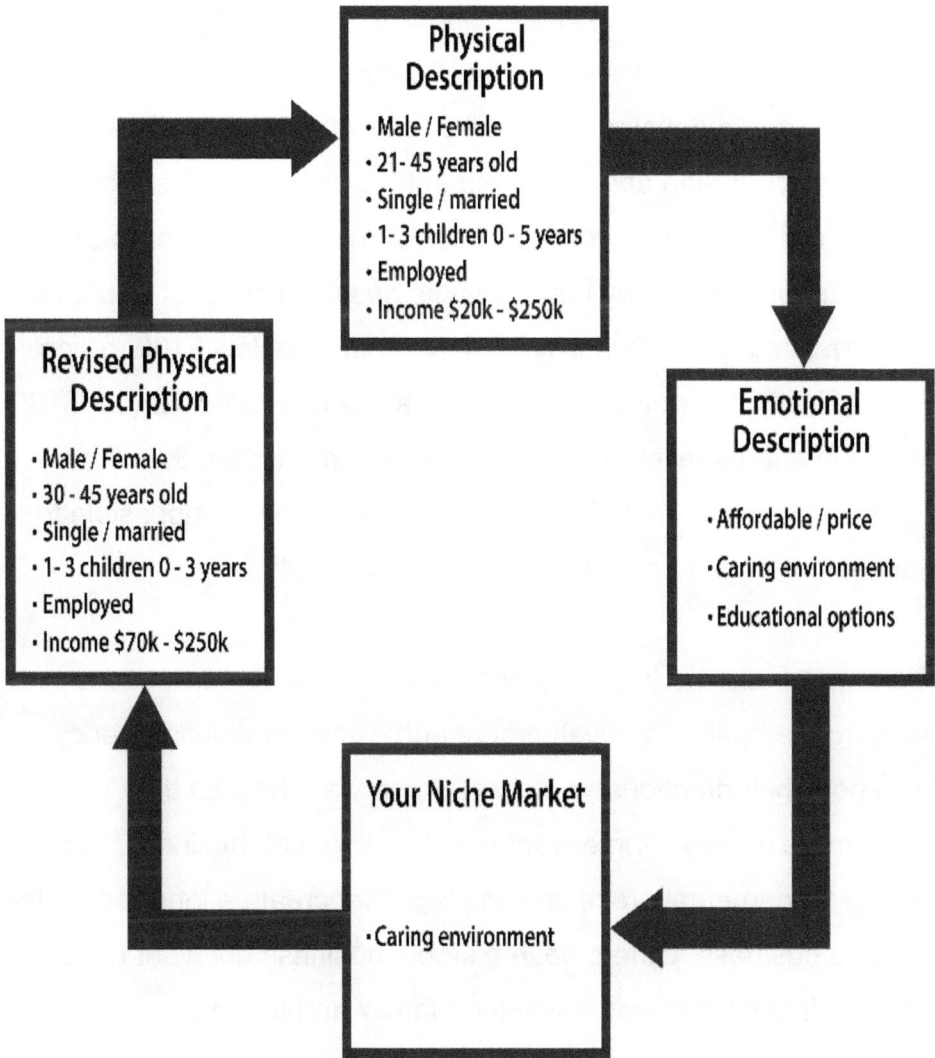

Physical Description

- Male / Female
- 21- 45 years old
- Single / married
- 1- 3 children 0 - 5 years
- Employed
- Income $20k - $250k

Emotional Description

- Affordable / price
- Caring environment
- Educational options

Your Niche Market

- Caring environment

Revised Physical Description

- Male / Female
- 30 - 45 years old
- Single / married
- 1- 3 children 0 - 3 years
- Employed
- Income $70k - $250k

This same situation applies to the business development and digital marketing agency. Their original physical profile included both business to business (B to B) and business to consumer (B to C) businesses. These businesses can be in start-up mode and developing but they want to develop at a much faster rate. They may be stuck at a specific plateau and want help getting unstuck or they may find themselves in serious economic trouble. They have fewer than twenty employees. They have a viable business concept or plan if they are starting up. Typically, their revenue is below $100 million. So physically, their universe is essentially any business under $100 million in annual revenue. Today, there are more than 30 million businesses in just the U.S. alone. It would be nearly impossible to market to that number of businesses successfully.

But emotionally, we know that more than 30 million businesses want from a business development and digital marketing agency. We know their emotional switches. Some want help so they can make more money. Some want help building their business and putting fundamental processes in place that create a long-term sustainable business. Others have a stable business but want to free up their time so they can enjoy their family and friends.

The business owners that want help to build their business are typically one to five years old. They have a single unit operation run by a solo professional operating as a LLC or sole proprietorship with $250,000 to $10 million in revenue and less than five employees. The ones looking to spend more time with their family are typically more than five years old with multiple units headed up by a CEO operating as either a C or S corporation with $10 million to $50 million in annual revenue and five to twenty employees; and the ones making 50 - 100 millions with more than 20 employees. Each of the three niche markets have a specifically defined physical profile and they both want what a business development & digital marketing agency sells.

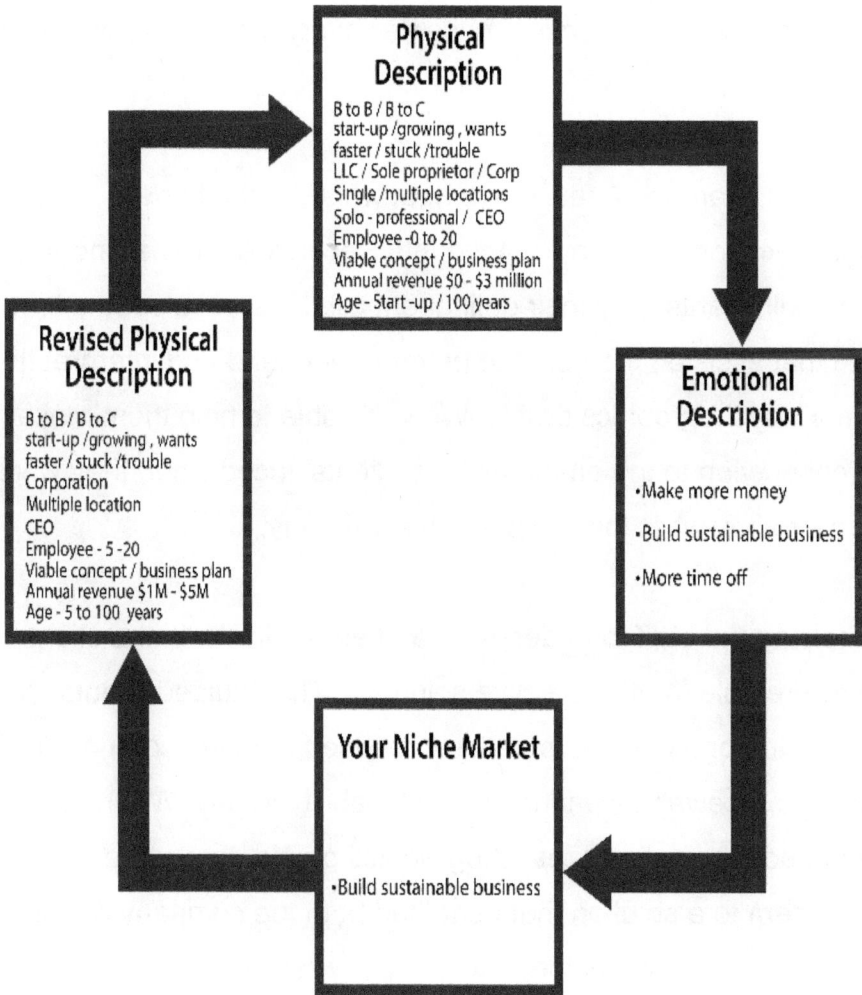

Physical Description

B to B / B to C
start-up /growing , wants
faster / stuck /trouble
LLC / Sole proprietor / Corp
Single /multiple locations
Solo - professional / CEO
Employee -0 to 20
Viable concept / business plan
Annual revenue $0 - $3 million
Age - Start -up / 100 years

Revised Physical Description

B to B / B to C
start-up /growing , wants
faster / stuck /trouble
Corporation
Multiple location
CEO
Employee - 5 -20
Viable concept / business plan
Annual revenue $1M - $5M
Age - 5 to 100 years

Emotional Description

•Make more money

•Build sustainable business

•More time off

Your Niche Market

•Build sustainable business

As a business owner, your job is to identify and define the most important emotional switches that apply to your business. Select only the one niche market that will serve your passion and revise your physical profile to define the prospects that make up that niche market. It all comes down to this: all prospects today want to feel special. They want to feel as though they're dealing with the expert that can help them solve their problems, concerns and frustrations once and for all. For the business that does this, your prospects will show up, pay you a premium price, tell everyone they know about you and never leave you.

Here's an example. A few years ago, we trained a huge communication company's Accounts Receivables department to "help their clients" pay their delinquent bills. We developed a template that assisted their staff to better understand and interpret their clients' psychographics profile. We were able to help them make the connection to the emotions their clients' faced when they were unable to pay what they owed to the company.

By helping the staff to understand and empathize with the clients, they were able to offer creative solutions. They guided clients through the process and creatively reduced both the company's accounts receivables and their client inability to pay. When they understood their clients' psychographics profile, they were able to direct them to a solution that benefited both the company and the client. In the end, we helped the company recover several hundred thousands in receivables.

The business that's unique offers exceptional and extraordinary value and clearly communicates these benefits as the unprecedented opportunity to totally and completely dominate their entire market. All you have to do is follow these steps to greatly increase your chances for success and use them in your marketing programs.

We want you to understand that building a million dollar business is not an impossible endeavor. It does require dedication and effort on your part. But if you follow the proven process we use with our clients, combined with a purpose and passion for what you do, you can do this, If you are serious and committed to building your business, then it is not an impossible task. Our intention is to equip you to achieve massive success in your business. It all starts right here with this book by developing your strategic position, your target customer profile and then working with the audience in which you specialize; your niche market.

Assignment

Now it's your turn. Find the revised form in your end of the section and transfer the information from your previous forms onto this new one. This will consolidate all your previous work into a single document you can access for review.

Record your original physical profile in the box at the top and your emotional profile in the box on the right. Place your niche market selection in the lower box, and then your revised physical information in the box on the left.

Let's quickly review what we've accomplished in completing your target customer profile. Our main purpose for this book is to help you develop the solid foundation required to build a highly successful business. That foundation demands that you know and understand the identity of your target customer.

We described the identification process by looking at the two major components that define your target customer; their physical profile or demographics and their emotional profile or psychographics.

Knowing your target customers' physical profile, while very important, only defines who needs what you sell. It identifies the physical characteristics of your target customer. The emotional profile identifies who wants what you sell. It identifies your target customer's emotional characteristic also known as their emotional switches.

When you know and understand their emotional traits, you also know and understand how to compel them to buy from you by appealing to their desires. By turning on their emotional switches, your prospects will pay attention to your message and want to buy what you sell because it brings them light. It solves the major problem, concern or frustration that may have consumed their lives.

By creating an accurate emotional profile, you completed a key step to eventually creating and developing a highly successful business. You create a unique business that provides exceptional and extraordinary value and effectively communicates its uniqueness and value to its prospects. The real key to creating this type of business is for you to review those emotional switches in your emotional profile and select just the one that most resonates with your purpose and passion. That selection becomes your niche market.

You will also convey this uniqueness in your marketing program. Your plan will generate real results and provide the powerful and compelling information you need to emotionally reach your prospects. Thanks to your niche market selection, you have identified qualified prospects who actually want what you sell versus those who just need what you sell. This dramatically narrowed the number of prospects that are available to buy your product or service. You will attract them because you have chosen to serve this niche market exclusively. By revising your original physical profile, you further refined the physical characteristics of your target customer so you know them when you see them. When it's time, you can find them and market to them.

Completing your target customer profile is a major step to also develop a long-term sustainable business that you can operate with total confidence and certainty. By the way, you've just completed a required basic business fundamental that 99.9% of all entrepreneurs and business owners never take the time or make an effort to complete. Congratulations on a job well done!

Next, we'll take a look at ways to help you innovate your business so you offer your prospects on-going exceptional and extraordinary value. You will then be well on your way to total and complete market domination. Just remember to transfer all your physical and emotional information to the revised form in the end of the section.

Select your niche market and record your choice in the lower box. Then complete this form by refining your physical profile on the left to fit your specific niche market. Keep in mind that each step we take continues to build on the previous ones, so take your time as you complete each assignment. Do your best because your business depends on it!

SECTION FIVE

Innovate

"The future belongs to those who prepare for it today."

- African Proverb

SECTION FIVE
Innovate

This last step of the five will focus on helping you to learn and understand how to innovate around what your target customer want and changes in how they make all important decisions about whether or not they will buy what you sell. Let's first consider a market survey of U.S. automobile buying patterns by J.D. Powers and Associates. It revealed that over one-third of all male car buyers deliberately visited their local dealership when it was closed so they could view the cars when no one else was around. Why would they do this?

Think about this for a moment. How much useful information can potential car buyer get pressing their nose again a display or peering through a chain link fence? Not, and yet average car salesperson honestly believes that their customers choose to purchase their next car based on a selection of features, like the way the car handles or gas mileage. These sales people have no clue that these traditional features are secondary considerations at best to the customer.

To the typical consumer, the purchase of a new car doesn't just mean a way to get around town. If they did, wouldn't everyone buy the next car based solely on price? And wouldn't the cheapest model be the world's market leader? All business owners and startups need to be aware of the fact that we decide to buy things based on emotion. We only use logic to justify our purchases.

When a customer buys a new car, they're looking for a certain feeling of satisfaction that exists within them. That new car represents something personal for them. They want their purchase to reflect whatever that feeling happens to be. A fast sporty-looking car may provide a perceived image of power, youth, adventure, and success. A hybrid or electric car may provide a perceived image of being forward-thinking, having freedom from high gas prices, having a conservative mindset, and easy mobility. The customer looking for the sports car will not buy a minivan. And the minivan buyer isn't interested in a compact car. This doesn't mean that facts never come into play.

Remember, we buy based on emotion but we justify our purchases with facts. As crazy as it sounds, most of us use facts to confirm choices we have already made. Facts validate the decisions we make every day. They come into play at the end of our buying experience instead of at the beginning. This may be the single biggest mistake most business owners make when they market their product or service. Very few customers make major buying decisions by creating a checklist of positive and negative attributes. We don't do it for the cars we drive, the friends we choose, the house we buy, or even the person we marry. We use the same process even on our chosen professions. This even includes fields like engineering and science which are fact-based. Not to forget even today in the digital world, the same principles apply. We follow and watch people on line based on our emotions.

In our day-to-day lives, we actually make very few decisions based on facts and figures. Instead, we rely mostly on senses. We match the things we experience and compare them with familiar past patterns that our collective experiences tell us meet our needs. Even search engines leverage on this human behavior and give us results or offer ads during our searches. When people move, they tend to gravitate towards neighborhoods that mirror their values and behaviors. While driving, we even prefer music that reminds us of our youth. We do this because it creates a familiar emotional response of feeling.

We certainly couldn't function at all If we had to analyzo every decision as if it was new. We just don't have the time or mental bandwidth. Our thought process has been honed over a thousand centuries of human evolution, enabling us to instantly assess new situations as either potentially dangerous or desirable. We have an almost instantaneous ability to unconsciously recognize certain patterns that aid us in making quick decisions.

Did you know that 90% of all new product advertising fails despite being market-tested in advance? That's because this testing uses logic-based approaches, like consumer surveys and focus groups. But we don't make our buying decisions based on logic. People make decisions based on emotion. In other words, they buy what they want, not just what they need. As of this writing, a brand of Lamborghini Aventador costs over $400,000 to buy. And yet, there's not one person on the planet who needs a Lamborghini. But there are a lot of people who want one. This is the reason Lamborghini stays in business.

That's why we repeatedly stress that in order for any business to be successful, you must stand out from the crowd. You must offer exceptional and extraordinary value. You must have a compelling message that lets your target customer know that your product or service is different from all others in that market and that you offer them so much value that they would be missing out to buy from anyone else.

We previously discussed selecting a specific target customer and focusing in on what they specifically want. This is often referred to as selecting a niche market. When you stop trying to market to every person who may need what you sell and instead focus on select customers who want a specific solution to a specific problem, you immediately stand out from the crowd. You will then quickly dominate this entire market.

Prospects want to deal with the expert. And for the savvy business owner or entrepreneur willing to break from the pack and market to specific segment of a much larger market, the prospects interested in what they sell will be instantly drawn to them. But you can't stop there. Your competition will quickly see what you're doing, and they will move in on your newly formed area of expertise. That means that you must innovate your business by adding products or services that give so much value that your prospects can't go anywhere else.

Innovate Your Business

This section will show you how to specifically define what your prospects want. We'll show you how to innovate everything in your business. This means that when your target customer is looking for a solution to their problem or frustration, they quickly discover that you offer a solution that blows away your competition.

We're going to walk you through the steps that will help you to identify once and for all exactly what your target customers want and the innovations that will position you as your market's top value provider. Always remember that your prospects do not buy price. They buy value. When you properly innovate your business, and you will never again compete on price. In fact, you can often raise your prices to the highest level in your industry. You can only do this when you take time to understand your ideal clients and offer them valuable services or products. So let's get started.

There are four simple stages that will quickly uncover what your target clients want. You can then innovate around that information.

In Stage One, you must try to see the world from your target customer's point of view. Try to mentally step into their shoes and visualize how they feel about their current situation. If you're a child psychologist and your target customer is a frustrated parent dealing with a screaming, hyperactive, uncontrollable child, then position yourself in the exact same situation and ask yourself, "If I were this parent, what would I want? What is my problem and what is the solution I want?"

If you're an employment screening company that specializes in performing background checks, and your target customer is a restaurant owner hiring new staff, what would they want? What hiring process challenges are they experiencing? What solutions rid them of these challenges? By stepping into the actual situation of the target customer, you can quickly get a feel for their anger, resentment, frustrations, and any other challenges they may be facing. Those emotions drive them to buy your products and services if what you offer provides the solution they seek.

That's the purpose of this book. In order to effectively market your product or service, you must understand the emotions of your target prospects. Those emotions drive them to seek out and pay for your solutions. That leads us to Stage Two. Once you identify what your target customers really want, you need to ask yourself if your business truly offers them what they want. The child psychologist's target customer wants their child to stop yelling and screaming. The psychologist must then offer a solution that quickly gives the customer exactly what they want.

The restaurant owner wants a speedy and safe way to check out the qualifications of new job applicants. The screening company must then offer a solution that does exactly that. But here's an important point to remember as you go through this exercise for your own business or business to come. Typically, your business will offer a solution for the vast majority of the problems your target customer is experiencing. But if you examine your solutions closely, they're most likely the same solutions your competition offers. Since you both offer the exact same thing, value is now reduced to the business offering the lowest price.

Stage Three is perhaps the most important stage you will take as an entrepreneur, a business owner or start up. You must offer exceptional and extraordinary value to your prospects. The only way to consistently do this is to innovate your business. What can you do or provide that will be viewed by your prospects as going that extra mile. The child psychologist may offer a free one-hour child discipline session to the parent just to prove that the doctor's solution actually works. By offering this session, the doctor proves the value of their services before the prospect makes a commitment. The doctor has added tremendous value up front. The background screening company could offer the restaurant owner actual case studies where they worked with other restaurant owners. They could provide physical documentation on how their services saved those restaurant owners from a legal nightmare or helped them increase their short-term revenue and profits.

Innovation is creating new systems, enhancing existing systems, and doing things in a better way that have not been done before. You must innovate everything your business does because the goal is improvement. You obviously can't innovate everything at once. So, how do you decide which areas of your business to focus on immediately and which areas will you place on hold? That's the purpose of this section. It all comes down to the question of wants versus needs. Your customers buy what they want, not just what they need. This section helps you identify exactly what your target customers want. Innovate these areas first and your revenue will skyrocket.

The child psychologist may innovate their business by offering a proven and tested thirty-day process where other doctors in this field may typically require sixty days. Or the doctor is certain their services work long-term that they are willing to guarantee their results for an entire year instead of their peers who offer ninety days. The employment screening company may offer personality profile-matching along with their screening services. They may actually create the perfect candidate profile based on the specific job requirements then offer to test each applicant and provide a full screening report to the hiring company. Do you think many other screening companies will offer all these services? Probably not!

If we take at look at our Window Cleaning and Power Wash case study, we'll see that this business owner did just that. He innovated his window cleaning business by offering expected value to all of his customers. He not only cleans their windows until they're immaculate but he also cleans their screens, which are often dirtier than the windows. As an added bonus, his crews clean the filthy window tracks and in and outside sills that most likely never receive attention from the home owner. He could later include additional value added services. For example, he could automatically repair all damaged screens and provide a unique window glass coating that is guaranteed to keep windows spot-free for a minimum of five years. Imagine as a homeowner, you will never have to worry about dirty windows for at least five years. Who wouldn't want to hire a window cleaner that did all these things?

Now, you might believe that his offering would have had a negative impact on his repeat business. After all, when he guaranteed his customers won't need his services for at least five years, it might appear to be detrimental to his business. In reality, it actually increased his business. After reviewing his previous customer records, he discovered that his target customers regularly contacted him for additional window cleanings once every seven years. The new five year treatment offered him the perfect opportunity to start a customer continuity program.

By offering a five year warranty on his work, this established a deadline in the minds of his customers. They automatically assumed they needed to repeat the service at the five-year mark. He was able to easily enroll a very high percentage of his customers into a continuity program where he automatically would come back on the fifth anniversary and repeat the process. This dramatically increased his target customer's lifetime value. If you own a cleaning business, the guarantee period with the customer continuity program will require a study for your customer base before implementation of this innovation.

This is why you must select your niche market based on your purpose and passion. Innovation takes work and effort. It can't be done half-heartedly or haphazardly. If you choose your niche market based on your ability to make a buck, you won't have the internal desire or aspiration to continuously innovate your business. You will view each day as drudgery and you will do just enough to get by. But when you select your niche market based on what you're passionate about, you will discover that you can't wait to get to work every day. Because now, it's no longer work. It's play!

You view every day as a new challenge to provide better quality and service to your customers. You continuously look for new and innovative ways to improve what you do; the customer service you provide, the information you make available, or the personal help you offer your target customers. This is not work or extra effort for you because you love what you do and you want to continuously improve.

We daily see many entrepreneurs and business owners who have absolutely no passion for what they do. It's obvious to everyone that deals with them, especially to their prospects. They want to do just enough to get by. They constantly say things like, "Just tell me what I should do." They don't have the drive to look forward and ask themselves what they could do in their business to provide their prospects with the ultimate customer experience. Don't fall into this same trap.

This brings us to Stage Four. Once you innovate the areas of your business that create exceptional value, it's time to pile on the value even more by generating a list of the specific benefits your target customer will enjoy as a direct result of your innovations. The child psychologist would list the benefits such as; restore peace and quiet back into your home; eliminate stress in your life; regain your family's love and respect; and enjoy your time together each and every day. The screening company could list benefits such as; getting the right person in the right job every time; and reducing absenteeism, call outs and no-shows. These things would relieve the owner's stress and worry when it comes to staff attendance and performance.

Let's go back to our child care client, Right Time Kids and go through the entire process to show you exactly how this works and how it ties back to your target customer profile. We implemented the same approach with Wisdom Senior Care to transform the owner and business, by continually adding value both to their clients and caregivers.

Example of Innovation Process

Physically, we originally identified the ideal child care customers as either male or female, twenty-one to forty-five years old, single or married, one to three children between the ages of three months up to five years old. They would be employed outside the home and with an annual income somewhere between 20,000 and $250,000 per year. In other words, any human being with children under age six that works outside the home and doesn't have a friend or relative that can watch them during the day needs the services of a child care center.

But then we asked ourselves these questions; what do all those parents really want? What is their emotional profile? What are their emotional switches? What are their problems, the fears, the frustrations, or concerns they have as they begin to face the reality that their situation is forcing them to place their young children into the custody of strangers? What are they experiencing emotionally?

We said that some of them want affordable pricing. Some want a caring, loving environment. And others are looking for educational options. It's imperative that child care owners define each and every one of these niche market segments. Once they do, they must choose the one they're most passionate about providing. They must select the one niche market that they want to specialize in. Whichever niche market they select, they must look back at their original physical profile and revise any characteristics that may have changed.

As an example, let's say as a child care owner, you selected a caring, loving environment as your niche market. What would their revised physical profile look like? The genders, marital status, number of children, and employment status, all remain the same as the original profile. But notice what changes now. Providing child care with specialized services like a loving environment will be much more expensive than child care that offers basic babysitting services. A child care center that provides a loving environment will offer services such as a much lower staff to child ratio, a nutritionist preparing daily meals, mandatory staff training in safety, and frequent staff rotation. These things keep the staff mentally alert and prevent adult burnout when dealing with children. Instead of appealing to twenty-one to forty-five year-olds, a loving environment appeals to prospects who can afford to pay for these more expensive child care services. They will need to be earning a higher household income and their average age will reflect that increase.

The revised physical profile would be thirty to forty-five years of age. The age of the child now comes into question as well. Most parents want child care that offers a loving environment when their children are three months old up to three years old. That could be because this is considered the most critically emotional age range for children. So the physical trait changes somewhat from our original. The income level must now also be revised because this childcare type will be about twice as expensive as the affordable child care.

The annual income for this group is now 70,000 to $250,000. But it becomes clearer now you've identified these prospects and what they specifically want. You now understand the emotional switches that will affect their thought process. Remember, they buy based on emotion. So what emotions are at play that will have a tremendous impact on their thought process? That thought process will guide our innovation process matrix.

An innovation process matrix can help us map the stages for our business innovation. Let's quickly review this innovation process matrix in a form so you can see how it works. Refer to the end of

INNOVATION MATRIX

CHOOSEN MARKET:

What They WANT	
What You DO NOW	
What You COULD DO	
How Will They BENEFIT	

Let's use this innovation matrix to map out this process and apply it to our child care example. Let's assume we've chosen the customer category that wants their child to have a loving, caring environment. That's our chosen niche market. What would we want from a child care facility that specializes in providing this type of environment? Asking this question and imagining our own children attending this facility makes it fairly easy to create a list of our own desires. If you face challenges in creating your list, reach out to parents you know who may fit this profile.

For example, when it comes to a child care center providing a loving environment, here is how some parents may fill in column one, "I want to know that my child is safe and that the staff is paying very close attention to them." Would you agree that this is basically what's going through the mind of most parents? This is one of their major emotional switches. There may be others as well. For example, "I want staff members who don't get irritated or frustrated when dealing with children all day long. I want to know for sure that my child is being well cared for by competent staff members."

Remember how we keep repeating that emotional switches represent the problems frustrations, fears, and concerns your ideal clients typically experience when they consider buying what you sell? Would you agree these three desires fall perfectly into these categories? Don't these also seem like reasonable parental expectations as parents consider whether or not to place their child in a child care facility that specializes in providing a loving, caring environment? These are the issues they worry about. These are the issues that must be resolved before you will ever convince them to place their child in your center. And yet, what do the majority of child care facilities focus on? They say things like "We have convenient hours, modern facilities, the lowest prices." Those are low priorities for this parental group.

Most parents are not concerned about low prices and convenient hours. They want their specific fears and concerns addressed up front. Can you see the huge competitive advantage you gained over your competition by understanding the relevant desires of your prospects? So, when you complete the form for your business, try to discover as many of these relevant emotional switches as you can that impact your prospects and customers. Also be sure to arrange them in order of priority from most important to the least important.

Now that we've analyzed and defined our ideal client's emotional switches, we next want to see if we presently offer products or services that actually solve any of these desires. We need to compare the customer's emotional switches to the child care center's existing services to make sure what the center offers is a solution to each of the customer's switches. In order to help you stay in the proper mindset during this exercise, we recommend starting the sentence in column two with the word "we." What do we do at our childcare facility as we take into consideration what our target customers want? How does our center presently solve these problems, frustrations, fears, and concerns for our prospective customers?

In the first example in row one, we said parents want to know that their child is safe and that the staff is attentive. So the center owner, using the word we, would write the solution their center provides in column two that matches with that specific want in column one. For example, "We provide all parents with written monthly incident reports that occur with their child. In the second desire, we said parents want staff members who don't get irritated or frustrated when dealing with children all day long. So the center owner might write, "We rotate our staff members throughout the day to keep them fresh." Our third emotional listed switch says that parents want to know that their child is being well-cared for by competent staff members. "We contact all past employers and list references during initial hiring process."

This is pretty simple isn't it? First, we state the basic parental concerns when placing their child into child care that specializes in providing a loving, caring environment. Then we list the solutions our center presently possesses to address those concerns. If you find it difficult to think of various issues your prospects and customers want on your own, then simply ask them. Survey them and make sure you specifically know what they really want from your business. If you're just starting your business and you don't have any customers yet, focus your survey on potential prospects that may be considering your product or service. You might even survey someone who currently uses a competitor.

If you don't have any prospects, then survey friends, associates, or family members who are currently using or the past have used a similar product or service. This is research time well-spent, especially when you consider that very few business owners or start ups take time to perform this type of analysis. Just this one exercise can help you dramatically separate your business from your competition. This process can be applied even at a departmental level in any organization dealing with a different audience. For example, one of our clients, Wisdom Senior Care successfully used this system and performed this analysis for their clients and their caregivers.

The solutions we've listed in column two are good, but not great. In fact, as you review them, wouldn't you agree that the solutions we listed in column two look typically the same for this industry? They are probably being used by most child care competitors as well. That indicates that there's no real value being offered if your competition is already covering that. So let's change that.

Ask yourself, what could you do that would raise the bar so high and create such a unique value and extraordinary service that you automatically stand out from all the other child care centers in your area. This is where you will start cultivating a unique skill that every business owner or startup must possess, but few master. We want you to start thinking outside the box and create new, different, better, and more innovative ways to improve what you're already doing. If you have a team, make sure you involve your team in the thinking for this key row.

Let's brainstorm the various options that could help us innovate our child care services and take this to another level. And let's use the words "we could" to get us started our row three. We remind you to get creative and let your imagination run wild. And if we're going to get creative, we have to agree that no idea is a dumb idea. In fact, if at least 50% of the potential innovations you list in row three don't get close to the absurd, you're not trying hard enough

Just because you write something down doesn't mean you're committed to doing it. You won't be expected to immediately implement any of these ideas until you carefully analyze each one to make sure they create extraordinary value and that they offer a positive return on investment (ROI). Instead, just think of this as an ideas row of "what ifs" row. And you may be thinking, "Why bother to write down absurd and outlandish possibilities even if we know the cost would be prohibitive, or we know the idea would never work for the business".

Talking trash is something familiar to human nature. But just remind yourself when it comes to that the reason is fairly simple. An outrageous idea may just lead to new and innovative thoughts that could work for your business. Remember all innovators for ages were seen as crazy when they brought up their innovative ideas. They were only respected once they brought their ideas to life. Craziness is the daily life of innovators.

So let's come up with some potential innovations for our child care center. Let's start by going back to our first desire example of our ideal customer who wants to ensure that their child is safe and that the staff is paying very close attention to them. Right now, all we give them is a monthly incident report that isn't very compelling. But look very closely in column one, row one and really analyze what these ideal clients are saying here. They want to know for sure that their child is safe and that the staff is paying very close attention to them. How will that ever happen?

It's not enough for them that you offer assurances that safety and nurturing is happening in your center. And if you did offer them assurances, do you really think they would just believe you? Of course not! We want you to train yourself and your team to think like your prospects think. Put yourself literally into their same mindset. Pretend you have a child in child care right now and then mentally run through a typical day as one of these parents.

Here's what that situation would most likely look like. You drop your child off at child care every morning and then get back into your car and start driving to work. What do you think the typical parent feels during that drive? What are emotions they're experiencing? What emotions would you be experiencing if you were in that situation? As you're driving to work, you would most likely be feeling remorseful; maybe racked with guilt; frustrated, and having to face and endure a nearly unbearable emotional situation. You're wondering how your child is being treated when you're not there. Remember, our target customers want to be certain that their child is safe and that the staff is watching them closely. Being able to give your child a virtual hug would be a bonus for any parent.

That was our "I want" statement, defining the first emotional switch. These are the raw emotions associated with that trigger. We have discussed many times that your prospects buy based on emotion. It's critical that you flesh these emotions out and thoroughly understand them so you can create marketing messages that resonate with these emotional switches.

Most business owners want to only market the positive side of their product or service. That doesn't work. There's an old saying when it comes to selling, "An undisturbed prospect will never buy." Never forget that basic fundamental. You must understand the negative emotions that your prospects are experiencing and then offer them a solution that will eliminate those negative emotions. Most prospects would rather eliminate pain and get rid of frustrations than increase pleasure. Knowing this, we can now apply it to our prospective child care parents.

They are suffering greatly as they drive to work with all of these negative emotions and guilt leading the way. One thing that will overcome these negative emotions is for this child care center to somehow offer to position the parents as "a fly on the wall" of the facility. They must find a way to give the parents the ability to see what is really going on at this center. The parents must have this access whether they are at work or at home. The center must find some innovative way to make this happen.

Row three and the innovation process matrix serves that purpose. This is your innovation row. This is where you begin to brainstorm all the different possibilities you may or may not be able to provide to your prospects and customers. But you won't know if you can provide them with innovative solutions. You won't know if you don't write them all down on paper and analyze them. And remember, no idea is a dumb idea.

To begin each of your innovation statements, use the words "we could" so that you know you could eliminate a lot of the negative emotions your prospects are feeling. For the child care parents, you can give them the ability to physically see their child at the center and see how they feel about it. Pay attention to see if this innovative idea goes way beyond the scope of your current row two solution, which was simply handing a parent a written monthly report. You could see if it's feasible to install a 24 hour camera surveillance system that allows parents to log on to a password-protected website and observe their child during the day from either work or home. Make sure that the system you choose guarantees that the children video data is secured on a cloud server that they can instantly access from any device.

If you were a parent with a child in child care, at this information age, how would you feel if you discovered you had the ability to log on to this pass word protected, 24 hour system?. From the day care website, you can see exactly what your child is doing and how they are being treated any time you chose. Would you feel less guilty when you log on to that site and saw for yourself firsthand that the staff is actively playing and entertaining your child. Would all of your negative emotions suddenly disappear as you personally witnessed your child laughing, squealing, and having the time of their life?

Of course they would! And when that happens, do you think these parents would ever consider changing to another child care provider? Would they likely begin to tell others about your child care, recommending you to family, friends, and work associates in the area? Would they be willing to provide you with testimonials? Would they gladly pay additional fees to have access to this type of service? Can you see how just this one innovation begins to help this child care center separate their business from all of their competitors? Can you also see how this innovation provides this child care center with a huge marketing advantage? They can now market this additional benefit as a standard part of the service they provide for all their customers.

This one innovation increases the value of the service they provide and allows them to charge more than their competition. Are you beginning to see why we said this section, when done properly, may help you to forever revolutionize your business? Please remember that in this innovation section, the child care owner is only writing down possibilities related to his or her niche market. That doesn't mean they're committing to implementing any of them. In fact, before they implement any of their ideas, they should first review the costs associated with making those changes versus the projected revenue increases they could charge by implementing them.

But we think you get the idea. In the case of this child care center, they may elect to charge a monthly fee for access to their 24 hour service, or they may elect to provide it to all parents (and incorporate the cost in their fees) knowing that it will generate a flood of referrals and new business. This will all depend on the business system you decide to put in place to support your innovation.

Let's take a look at our second prospects desire example. In row two, column one, it says that the parents want staff members who don't get irritated or frustrated when dealing with children all day. Our current solution is to rotate our staff members throughout the day to keep them fresh. That's okay, but it's not compelling and doesn't get noticed. It doesn't stand out from what other child care facilities may also be providing. So let's brainstorm. What if we could lower our staff to child ratio from our present eight to one down to a five to one ratio. We could also add that our staff will spend additional quality time with the children every day. Doesn't that sound more compelling to parents?

Our third prospect desire example says that the parents want to ensure that their child is being well cared for by competent staff members. Our current solution is to contact all past employers and listed references during the initial hiring process. But what if we could perform annual background checks and random drug screenings four times per year on all staff members? Doesn't that sound much more impressive and reassuring to parents considering child care than simply telling them we contact all past employers and list of references during the initial hiring process?

That's all there is to this. Pretty simple, isn't it? And remember; when you begin to create innovative ideas, there are no wrong answers. You're simply analyzing what each emotional switch means from your target customer's point of view. And if you get stuck on one or two of the emotional switches and can only come up with a single potential innovation, that's okay. It may take only a single innovative idea to revolutionize your business. And we remind you once again of this very important point; there are no dumb ideas. Write down whatever ideas come to mind, no matter how crazy they may initially seem.

But wait. We're still not done. Remember how we're using this innovation process matrix to help you uncover the emotional components of your prospects? Do you also remember that benefits tap into the emotions of your prospects but features tap into their logic? You want to make sure you define the specific benefits your prospects will receive from every innovation you record in row three. This will provide you with additional guidance when the time comes for you to decide which innovations to use. We designed row four in your innovation process matrix to help you capture that information. So in row four, you must make sure you list the benefits for each innovation you list in row three. You can use those listed benefits in your marketing messages in such a way that you get your target customers to notice and respond to you.

In our child care case study example, when parents used the 24 hour web service system to view for themselves that the staff members are providing a loving, caring environment, the benefits to the parents would sound like this: "Your child will be made to feel at home and treated as if they were our own child. Our daycare parents feel enormous relief and experience complete confidence and certainty knowing that their child is receiving the finest child care available. Our parents also feel like they're in control. They have increased peace of mind and no longer experience concern and worry about staff competence and safety." You can actually use your business name or day care name if this relates to what you do by adding your special touch to it.

Are you starting to see why this works and why these simple exercises produce multimillion-dollar businesses? Do you think any other business owner or entrepreneur goes through similar exercises? We guarantee you that many business owners don't go through this exercise. In fact, most businesses only compete on price. You will never have the business of your dreams if you're forced to compete on price.

If you were a child care center owner, you would want a facility that competes on value. Most prospects are more than willing to pay a much higher price if they see additional value in what you offer. In our childcare example, if you were a parent, would you pay more money for a facility that offers a lower staff to child ratio or that offers parents a way to see their child online any time they choose? What parent wouldn't want that? This all depends on you knowing the identity of your target and niche market.

Assignment

So now, it's your turn to apply this to your business. This works well for profit or non profit businesses. We've included forms in the end of the section of this book to accompany you and help guide you through this exercise. Just follow these examples we have provided, and you will begin to fully understand the process to always innovate for your target customers. Use the process to differentiate your business and dominate your market place.

Let's quickly recap what we've accomplished in this last step of our 5 steps for market domination. Our main purpose is to help you develop a solid foundation to differentiate your business and make it highly successful. That foundation demands that you know and understand the identity of your target customer. And then to immediately understand the process of how that customer makes decisions about whether they will buy what you sell.

The innovation process matrix in this section will help you discover this by, first, defining the problems, frustrations, fears, and concerns your target customer typically faces when they do business with your industry. Second, you want to verify that you do indeed currently offer a solution that eliminates that problem forever from your target customers' lives. Third, look for potential innovative solutions that create massive value for your target customers and completely separate your business from all of your competitors.

And fourth, write out all the benefits those innovations will provide to your target customers.

Never forget that innovation is the key to success for any business owner. So take your time and create and explore as many innovative solutions as you can. Just be sure they're based on the specific things your target customers want or desire. Make it all but impossible for them to not do business with you. Create a situation where they literally say to themselves that they would be missing out to buy from anyone else but you. If you continually do this, you will forever dominate your market.

To close this book, your target customers want to feel special. They want to feel as though they're dealing with the expert that can help them solve their problems, concerns, and frustrations once and for all. They want a business that does things differently from everyone else who offers a similar product or service. They want a business that stands out from the crowd. They want a business they feel truly understands them, caters to them, and offers them exceptional value.

But here's the great news. When they do find you, they're willing to pay a higher price to get this special treatment. As long as they receive the value perceive they'll receive exceeds the price they'll pay. For the business that does this, market domination is all but ensured. Prospects begin to appear almost out of thin air. They will begin to pay top price. They will insist on telling everyone they know about the exceptional value you provide to every customer you serve.

And best of all, they will never leave you for a competitor; even a much cheaper one. You can convey all of these benefits to your target customer throughout your marketing program. You can use these benefits to generate real bottom line results by structuring powerful and compelling information you uncover in this exercise so you can emotionally market to your prospects.

Our primary goal in this book is to help you strategically yet effectively apply the basic business fundamentals required to build a sustainable and scalable million-dollar business. But it starts by positioning and differentiating your business from your competition in these five easy steps in the five sections in this book. These steps are from our experiences and life principles of our human nature.

The business owner and entrepreneur's journey is a roll coaster ride. The fun is higher if you are equipped and have the right support during the journey. It is okay to look for professional help when overwhelmed. Savvy and informed business owners understand that time allocation requires them to get more out of their twenty-four hour day. They can do this with qualified help. Business owners can then focus on what is important. It is critical to bring in qualified customers and trusted accountability partners to keep them moving forward. For more than a decade, wEquipu team has been working with business owners worldwide. You can be part of this network of business owners who entrusts us with their business growth. We believe the tools in this book will give you guidance and support in building your business foundations. We hope it will strengthen your business and help you avoid being in business by yourself. Whether you are a brick and mortar business in your community or a digitally located business, our hope is that you enjoy your roller coaster journey to success!

ABOUT THE AUTHORS
Achille Nangbong B. Bomboma
Founder wEquipu

Fulbright Alumni, the United State of America Department noticed his works with Small and Medium sized Businesses in 2006. The opportunity allowed him to expand his business development skills in North America with Small and Medium Businesses. He and his business partner founded wEquipu, a business development and internet marketing agency, to equip Small and Medium Businesses on business growth principles and strategies.

Over the last 15 years, his professional life settings have afforded him the opportunity to assist various business owners learn, and improve their business management and performance. As a business growth catalyst and serial entrepreneur, he saved businesses in US, Canada and Africa an average of 45% on operating expenses and cash collections, increased sales by an average of 80% through business principles focused strategies.

His strong leadership skills, as well as ability to connect with inter-disciplinary team, position him for performing in different cultures and made him an open-minded and culturally competent person. He is a strong believer in developing countries development through the development of their Small and Medium Enterprises, and population health.

Christopher D. McMullan
Founder wEquipu

Proud exceptional Digital Marketer, he focused on creating high-performance marketing strategies that create positive ROI. His mission as Founder of wEquipu & SEO (Search Engine Optimization) expert is to maximize the volume of inbound organic traffic from search engines to businesses' website. He accomplishes this through a combination of on-page and off-page techniques, including link-building, social media strategy, viral marketing, metadata sculpting, site speed optimization, content strategy, information architecture, which has produced a measurable ROI and Page One listing on Google.

His focus is to help small businesses overcome fierce competition, modest budgets and solidifying their sales and marketing engine by improving lead generation, conversion rates and profits generation strategies. Develop end-to-end web solutions focused on Google Cloud Platform technologies. Oversee clients' SEO accounts, drive strategic SEO vision and integrate within internal/client design & development teams. Develop strategies for consumer's search behavior, analyzing competitors and leveraging those data points to inform client's content strategies.

As a result of the daily changes in the search algorithms of Google, Bing, Yahoo he is responsible of providing to clients the Skill Set needed in internet marketing.

To order additional copies and for more information contact our office.

Part of the proceeds of this book will go to international business educational projects. Contact our office for additional information.

info@wEquipu.com - https://wequipuseo.com -https://wequipu.com

www.ingramcontent.com/pod-product-compliance
Lightning Source LLC
Chambersburg PA
CBHW051826090426
42736CB00011B/1664